GOD

AND

RATIONALITY

GOD
AND
RATIONALITY

THOMAS F. TORRANCE

T&T CLARK
EDINBURGH

T&T CLARK LTD
59 GEORGE STREET
EDINBURGH EH2 2LQ
SCOTLAND

First published 1971 by Oxford University Press
First published in paperback 1997 by T&T Clark Ltd

ISBN 0 567 08582 1

British Library Cataloguing-in-Publication Data
A catalogue record for this book is available from the British Library

Printed and bound in Great Britain by Hartnolls Ltd, Bodmin

Memoriae
Caroli Barth
Doctoris Ecclesiae Universalis
Magistri Mei Cari
In Universitate Basiliensi

Preface

Today natural science is at work penetrating into the heart of the ultimate questions of the universe that carry it to the very frontier of created being, which it can approach but cannot cross by means of the methods it has developed. The closer to that boundary science is thrust, the more necessary it becomes for it to engage in serious dialogue with theology if it is to be at home in the whole domain of human knowledge. But is theology today capable of sustaining such a dialogue with the same kind of rigour and dedicated rationality found among natural scientists? Theology is doubtless the most difficult of all subjects, making immense demands upon our spiritual and mental powers. In it we have to struggle arduously and persistently with ourselves in order to develop a scientific inquiry in which we learn how not to project ourselves into the centre of the picture but rather how to allow the rationality of God to throw its masterful light upon the whole area of human experience and knowledge. Yet much contemporary writing in theology remains strangely shallow and lacking in metaphysical anguish. It is characterized by a marked reluctance to attempt the profound shift in the perspective of thought and language about God that is needed if theology is to be set back again on a sound scientific basis. Unfortunately, too many are bemused by the idea that theology can be renewed for our generation only by returning to ordinary language and reinterpreting everything in terms of current fashion and popular opinion. What they often succeed in doing, however, especially in their appeal to the 'non-conceptual' and 'non-objective', is to offer modern man, over-anxious about his own lack of maturity and wisdom, a kind of tranquillizer, through disconnecting the surface of his religious life from the rational depths of his existence in God. Far from touching the real problems in religious need, this only serves to reinforce the blockage in people's relation to God and to contribute to the emergence of autistic people suffering from religous aphasia.

Despite this judgement about modern popular theology, I believe that in its main development Christian theology is engaged in a very far-reaching movement of advance in which we are able to discern a basic logical unity emerging out of a synthesis between the past and the present. Many lines of thought are now converging together in such a way that irrelevant structures are beginning to disappear and genuine structures are settling more securely upon their permanent foundations. A scientific theology of this kind resting on its own rational grounds is far more relevant to fundamental science in every area of human experience than most people realize. Without the clarification of our knowledge of the Creator, which it is the business of theology to undertake, we shall never be able to reach the overall rational unity in understanding for which the specialized sciences are grasping, but it is only when theology is pursued as a pure science for its own sake, or rather for the sake of God Himself, that its intellectual beauty is properly unveiled.

The intention of this book is to call for a return to theological rationality, and in particular to challenge younger theologians, who can measure up to the rigorous training and discipline it demands, to get down to the hard work of developing the refined cognitive instruments adequately matched to the subject-matter, of which theology stands in such great need, but to which even our most illustrious predecessors have given so little consideration. This is also an evangelical task, for we will never be able to urge knowledge of God in Jesus Christ upon a world increasingly dominated by science unless we can commend it upon its own adequate scientific basis.

I should like to acknowledge my indebtedness to Gottlob Frege, Friedrich Waismann, and Albert Einstein, who have taught me much from their writings about co-ordinating reflection with the realities we experience, and not least to Karl Barth, the one theological giant of the modern era, yet the humblest inquirer of the living God. It is in thankfulness to him, whose immense service to Christian theology terminated a few days ago, that these pages are dedicated.

Many readers may find it helpful to begin with the second and third chapters or with the last chapter, and then to return to the introductory chapter before proceeding to the rest of the book, although the philosophical and scientific theologian will doubtless prefer to begin with 'Theological Rationality'. Since this book is designed to accompany *Theological Science* and *Space, Time and Incarnation*, may I direct readers to those books for the treatment of some questions which they may miss here?

While I am much in debt to a host of others in the preparation of these books, my essential indebtedness is to my dear wife, Margaret, without whose selfless love and godly wisdom any work of mine would be immeasurably poorer.

Christmas, 1968   THOMAS F. TORRANCE
Canty Bay, East Lothian.

My two sons, Thomas and Iain, have given me considerable help at a very busy time in the correction of the proofs and in the preparation of the index, for which I am most grateful, but I owe them more than I can say for the discerning and helpful comments they constantly offer out of their own philosophical studies.

My cordial thanks are also due to Mr. Geoffrey N. S. Hunt and his colleagues in the Oxford University Press for the patience and precision of their service in the processes of publication.

June 1970   T.F.T.
New College, Edinburgh.

Preface to the New Edition

This book was originally published to follow up *Theological Science* and *Space, Time and Incarnation*, in order to reinforce the view that theology is a science in its own right, operating with a basic form of rationality governed by its proper object. This calls for renewed appreciation of the positive kind of rationality pursued in rigorous science, in relation to which authentic Christian theology is to be pursued in developing positive modes of thought matched to the subject-matter rather than in accordance with subjective cultural trends. A theology ground in Jesus Christ the incarnate Son of God cannot but be intensely personal but it is not subjective. In all rigorous science it is only the person who can engage in objective operations, but in Christian theology it is the person healed and made whole through Christ who thinks from a centre in Christ and not in himself. This calls forth from us deeper thinking about the obedience of the mind to its divinely given object, which is what *dogmatic* in the proper sense really means.

Easter, 1997   T.F.T.
Edinburgh.

Contents

I INTRODUCTION

I

Theological Rationality

In recent decades theology has been harassed by the imperialism of mechanistic concepts emanating from a dogmatic scientism and a dogmatic empiricism, end-products of the Newtonian era of science. In reaction some biblical scholars and theologians have allowed themselves to be driven into existentialism and phenomenology where they have been caught in the flight from scientific objectivity, only to founder in the morass of historical relativism in which Jesus, in spite of desperate attempts to hold on to Him, keeps vanishing from their instruments of observation. Others have taken refuge in cultural expressionism and sociology where they are stranded in the yawning gap between modern culture and historic Christianity, in which God interpreted as a function of man's ultimate social concern keeps dying out on them. Multitudes of Christian people now find themselves in the wilderness of irrationality and confusion.

The immediate reason for this in the Church is the deep cleavage that has opened up between theology and experience. Detached from the empirical reality of the living and acting God, theology tended to become abstract and rationalistic and got stuck in arid ideas and inflexible frames of thought, losing its relevance for the life of faith. The estrangement of theology from its proper object meant also its estrangement from the common man. On the other hand, the Church, giving itself out as the patron of experience, tended to develop first a pragmatic ideology of its own existence and then a sort of religious technology for its mission in place of theology, throwing up ethico-social and ecclesiastical structures in which many people have felt so restricted and stifled that everywhere among them there is growing revolt against what they choose to call 'the establishment'. There is thus real ground for disillusionment. If theology without experience is irrelevant and experience without theology is blind, the Church without theology can be little more than a blind leader of the blind. Yet the real cause of the trouble does not lie with theology or the Church as such, but with the rift between the spiritual and the physical that has come to affect both and which is a reflection in them of the disastrous dichotomies between thought and life, reason and behaviour, law and nature, found in our modern culture. Theologies that take shape within these divisions tend to operate with such a disjunction between God and the world that they fail the everyday experience of the believer, for they are not grounded in the actual understanding of faith that arises out of man's reciprocal relations with God and are therefore unable to minister rationally to his communion with God. Their statements are found in the last analysis to be empty of objective content and inevitably run out into meaninglessness—that is why they are such easy prey to the logical empiricists and verificationists.

However, the state of affairs I have been describing is a transitory phenomenon, the sort of thing that has characterized theological development from time to time in the past when the whole perspective of human thought was on the move. Theology can never operate outside the historical situation and therefore cannot but be conditioned by the notions and tools which it uses from age to age. But as these major mutations in the orientation of thought take place, theological formulations are shaken up, and there is a loosening of the relation between the fundamental datum of theological knowledge and the moulds of traditional thought and language in which it has come to be expressed. Frequently this results in an interim period of confusion, but, to judge from the past, this can have the effect of isolating pseudo-theological factors and throwing theology back upon its proper foundations where it can become geared in again to the intelligible structure of the object of knowledge and so find profounder renewal. That is, I believe, what is happening today; but it is a crucial period for theology. If, overcome by anxiety, it tries to eke out a sort of beleaguered existence by retreating into the dim light of 'non-objective' truth or into the refracted light of 'paradox', it will be quite fatal. No form of knowledge can survive or maintain its impact on mankind that tries to keep alive by taking cover from the searching light of scientific inquiry. If theology is to survive the crisis of these times, it must move out into the full light of day, engage in critical revision of its own theoretic framework, and go on to fresh scientific construction under the pressure and determination of its own object.

This does not mean that theology must always start *de novo* in the present, cutting itself adrift from the past and treating its historic formulations as if they were devoid of any essential relation to the substance of the faith and could be discarded without much regret, like outworn clothing. Doubtless, if through historical analysis of the conditions underlying the shaping of those formulations the substance of the faith at which they aimed becomes clearer to us in its instrinsic intelligibility, not a few formulations will be judged expendable in the light of it. But in so far as we are now able through prior formulations to apprehend the objective reality in a greater fullness than they could specify at the time, the basic concepts and relations they involve will accredit themselves to us as rooted in the structure of reality and therefore as belonging to the essential content of the faith. Far from being discarded they will be thought out afresh, assimilated in a deeper and wider understanding of the faith, and thus be secured as permanent theological gains. In this way fundamental truth appropriated and formulated long ago continues from the past into the present, more surely and richly disclosed because of its passage through different perspectives and critical stresses in human understanding, and at the same time more relevant to us today because of its detachment from the presuppositions with which it had come to be overlaid and obscured.

It is always a hazardous undertaking to loosen our bonds with the great achievements of the past, but unless we learn how to forget as well as how to remember we will not be able to achieve any new insight or advance in understanding. What is constantly

needed, however, is a disciplined penetration into the inner intelligibility of the faith, enabling us to distinguish time-conditioned
images and representations from the substance of the faith, and to
determine which concepts and relations can be justified and re-
tained. This is a critical task which the theologian must undertake
for himself, and which he cannot afford to leave to the phil-
osopher, since it is the theologian who really knows how far concepts and relations actually match the object of his knowledge.
Hence he must develop, like the physicist, his own meta-science
or critical and epistemological clarification of his basic concepts,
if he is to give the faith compelling expression in the thought-
world of today with its roots secured in the permanent theological
gains of the past and the ground cleared for decisive advance
in the future. It is, I believe, through a sustained integration
of theological reflection with its proper object and a rigorous
development of its own field of rational activity in this way that
theology can maintain its integrity in the changing climate of
human thought. This is nothing else than a demand for scientific
theology operating on its own ground, and engaging in active
dialogue with the natural human sciences, in its own distinctiveness.

In order to introduce the discussion in the succeeding chapters,
let us consider now something of what is needed if this demand
is to be met.

I A MORE ADEQUATE CONCEPTION OF SCIENCE

It is surprising to find how many theologians, and not merely the
popular sort, still hold the obsolete notion of science as detached,
disinterested knowledge concerned only with observable things
and processes that can be analysed and defined in clear-cut ideas
and rigid structures, and computed so precisely that their various
states can be plotted in advance. This is the instrumentalist and
mechanistic view of science in which we claim to know only
what we can control, and accept as valid only what can pass the
test of our predictions. If that is what is called 'objective' knowledge, then it is not surprising either that they should reject the
concept of scientific theology and prefer to place theology in some
realm of 'non-objective' knowledge.

Of course, it is quite true that we do not act upon God as an object! The object of theological knowledge is not some manipulable thing that can be subjected to experimental tests of our own contriving in order to force the truth out of it. That is not at all how we can treat the living God or determine His transcendent reality, for He cannot be brought within the objectifying moulds of our prescriptive structures or netted within the devices of 'our science'. But if that is what 'science' is about then it would be very difficult today to point to any field of reality which was accessible to scientific knowledge in this way. The truth of the matter is that this is a very 'old hat' notion of science going back to Haeckel and even to Laplace who quite arbitrarily treated a rigidly mechanistic concept of physics as the model of all true science. It is easy to understand the rise and spread of this idea in view of the extraordinary success of celestial mechanics from the time of Galileo and Newton, but the persistence of this view, with its hard concept of determinism and idealization of mechanical explanation, after the emergence of quantum mechanics and the breakdown of the old principle of causality, is a strange anachronism. It is at such a point as this that historical analysis of the development of scientific and philosophical ideas helps to lift our thought out of the hardened ruts in which it had been moving, and enables us to recover rational freedom.

With the profound change that has now come about in the structure of modern science, e.g. with the relativity theory, thought is pushed beyond the boundaries of the observable and picturable, but this has meant (in Heisenberg's language) the renunciation of the criterion of perceptibility, or at least a severe limitation in its range of applicability. Similar treatment is also accorded to the criterion of predictability. Of course its range had never been so wide as many people would have us believe. There is no place, for example, for prediction in Kepler's laws or Darwin's theory, not to speak of history.[1] But it is now clear that prediction is applicable only within certain limited brackets where we are concerned with determinate aspects of nature alone, and that even there

[1] Cf. M. Polanyi, *The Logic of Liberty, Reflections and Rejoinders* (Routledge and Kegan Paul, London, 1951), p. 16.

prediction is not applied to the relation of events with events as such but to abstractions from our observations or to our theoretical constructions. Nevertheless it cannot be used to define a hypothesis which is compounded of open questions organized along the line of some discernible clue and then put to nature in the hope that it will yield an answer which we could not actually predict, for if we could we would not be learning anything really new but only inferring something from what we already knew. Prediction has its place only in argument within a closed system or from fixed premises, physical or conceptual, but the more open a science is the less will be the emphasis laid upon it.[1] It is thus quite wrong-headed to make prediction the hall-mark of all true science, in fact as impossible as it is to reduce inductive processes to transformations in accordance with logical rules.

What then becomes of the notion of scientific 'detachment' so exalted in the nineteenth century? Today this appears rather pathetic, for our psychology insists that detachment is not the sign of rationality but of open-mouthed imbecility![2] Applied to science of course, the notion goes back to the unfortunate Cartesian split between subject and object, in which the observing and thinking subject was thrown back upon himself as the one centre of certainty in a sea of doubt. Thus it was put abroad that scepticism belongs to the essence of the scientific attitude. Actually, however, doubting questions are not at all the same as scientific questions. The scientist does not doubt the object of his inquiry, for he is committed to a profound belief in its intelligibility, otherwise he would not be involved in its investigation. What he does subject to doubt are his own assumptions about the object, and so he allows attachment to the object to help him detach himself from his own presuppositions. He directs open questions to the object in order to let it disclose itself to him in its own reality and nature, and in the light of what he learns he revises his questions in order

---

[1] Cf. Popper's discussion of the logical distinction between routine and conjectural prediction, *Conjectures and Refutations* (Routledge and Kegan Paul, 1963), p. 117f.

[2] See M. Polanyi, *The Logic of Liberty*, p.25, and the *Tacit Dimension* (Routledge and Kegan Paul, London, 1967), p. 78f.

that his interrogation may be nearer the mark, but all this has the effect of calling in question the preconceived ideas of the investigator himself. Because ultimately he cannot disentangle his questions from their roots in himself, the questioner, or from their shaping in the structure of his own thought and existence, he finds himself being questioned down to the very roots of his being. That is why the scientist, far from being disinterested in his inquiry, is passionately involved, for what is at stake is the integrity of his own rationality vis-à-vis the relentless compulsion upon him of the inherent rationality of the universe, i.e. what we call the scientific conscience.

This is another way of speaking about scientific *objectivity*, which it would be as irrational to deplore as it would be to engage in objectless thought, while to identify objectivity with objectification would be a serious confusion. Objective thinking certainly involves the disciplined control of our subjectivities lest they should be unwarrantably obtruded upon the object of inquiry and thus allowed to obstruct and distort apprehension of it. This does not mean that once again the knowing subject is detached from the object of its knowledge, but rather that it enters into a close and active engagement with it, prepared and ready for whatever it may reveal in the give-and-take of investigation. Hence objective thinking lays itself open to the nature and reality of the object in order to take its shape from the structure of the object and not to impose upon it a structure of its own prescription. Objectifying or object-making thought, however, is the antithesis of this, for in it we 'make and mould' our objects of knowledge out of the stuff of our consciousness. It is the activity in which a thing is 'known' only as it is coercively grasped and projected as an 'object' through an inflexible conceptual structure which, whether in its Newtonian or Kantian form, is regarded as conditioning the thing and establishing it as a knowable reality. Since this structure is not a determination of experience but is independent of it, it is beyond the possibility of criticism or modification by experience. Through it, therefore, objectifying thought imports a powerful element of subjectivity into the object and thereby necessarily limits the possibilities of knowledge in an arbitrary way. This means that no advance to radically new knowledge can take place without a profound change in the structure of the scientific consciousness, a change in which a frame of thought basically correlated with the subject is turned inside out and correlated instead with the object, i.e. when objectifying thinking gives way to objective thinking.

It is unfortunate that while physicists and mathematicians have long since learned to distinguish between objectivity and objectification, too many theologians still tend to identify them, revealing how much they are still stuck in eighteenth- and nineteenth-century concepts. Emancipation from rigid structures is to be achieved, not by rejecting objectivity but by entering into the rational freedom that comes with objectivity and its detachment of thought from arbitrary control by subjective factors. Objectivity in theological science, like objectivity in every true science, is achieved through rigorous correlation of thought with its proper object and the self-renunciation, repentance and change of mind that it involves.

It is a more adequate understanding of science that will help to deliver theologians from their fear of it. Science is nothing more, as Einstein has said,[1] than the refinement of everyday thinking, for it respects the fundamental nature of things and seeks to understand and explain them in their own intelligibility. It is the essence of science, then, to bring together the theoretical and the empirical, and to let empirical relation to the object determine the mode of rationality we must adopt toward it, in order that we may coordinate and deepen our experience. This means also that the concepts of science are not used prescriptively, for they are developed out of a reciprocal connection between reflection and reality so that their material content is derived from the empirical realities to which they refer. This is not to say that in any science we can determine precisely how concepts are co-ordinated with experience, but it does mean that we can engage in science only through a profound faith in the accessibility of things to rational understanding. To cite Einstein again, 'the eternal mystery of the world is its comprehensibility.'[2] True science in every field of knowledge

[1] *Out of my Later Years* (The Philosophical Library, New York, 1950), p. 59.
[2] Op. cit. p. 60.

is science that stands in awe of that mystery, and that is the kind of science with which we are concerned in theology.

2 A MORE ADEQUATE SENSE OF CONNECTION

The ability to think can be spoken of as the ability to connect things up with other things and to think their interrelations. Hence it is important for correct thinking to determine the specific mode of connection or the kind of relation that obtains between the things we are contemplating. Correspondingly, science can be described as the activity in which we investigate things and events for the order or regularity they manifest in their inter-connections in the attempt to reduce the manifold of relations in the world, or at least in some field of experience, to some kind of uniformity, and if possible to penetrate down to a unitary logical basis in our understanding of them through which the whole field of our experience can be illuminated. Moreover, since we are not con-concerned in science merely with theoretic relations but with the co-ordination between the theoretical and the empirical, we cannot proceed very far without elucidating the distinctive nature of the connection that obtains in each field of inquiry, for it would only sidetrack scientific thought to clamp down upon experience a system of relations alien to it. Nevertheless, this is precisely what science is constantly tempted to do through its methods of abstraction and formalization. In the process of abstracting forms from its observations and organizing them into a symbolic system as a primary instrument of thought, science can become so confined within it that it has difficulty in rising above it and then tends to substitute a rigid system of formal relations for dynamic interconnections between actual events. This is what happened, for example, in the idealization and universalization of causality, together with the kind of logic that went with it, and its imposition upon every area of reality (which inevitably helped to promote the confusion between objective and objectifying thought).

Now, however, modern science has forced us to question both the adequacy of the causal relation and its application to all human experience. Thus in the development of nuclear physics scientists had to break free from the hard mechanical concepts of classical physics, limiting and modifying the basis of their application by throwing their thought into different but co-ordinated levels of connection. It was realized that while causal connection in the pre-quantum sense obtains in the setting up of an experiment, 'it does not follow', as Waismann has put it, 'that it must also apply to the hidden reality which manifests itself in the experiment'.[1] In quantum mechanics, however, a different kind of connection came to view which could not be construed in terms of the old principle of causality on the model of classical mechanics without absurd contradictions, and which required a radical reconstruction in the logical basis of scientific thought for its rational apprehension. This is the so-called 'uncertainty relation' which, it seems to me, it would be a mistake to speak of as 'indeterminacy' for that would still be trying to construe it by reference to the model of classical determinism. To insist that everything be interpreted on the same level of connection leads to a downright impasse in a conflict between the logic in which the classical understanding of connection has been formalized and the rationale of the behaviour of quanta. To cite Waismann again, 'If logic is right quantum theory must be wrong, and if quantum theory is right (in particular the uncertainty relation), then classical logic must be wrong (in particular the law of excluded middle).'[2] This is why various scientists in our day have been trying to elaborate a new kind of logic on different levels, sometimes called 'quantum logic', in order to give appropriate and adequate rational expression to the distinctive kind of connection between the geometrical and dynamic aspects of reality that concerns us here.

While this does not immediately affect theology, it is nevertheless highly instructive for it to learn that physics, in which one might have expected logico-causal relation to be immutably entrenched, has had to break free from it under the pressure of empirical relation to its object and has had to operate with a different kind of connection more adequate to the nature and reality of

[1] *How I see Philosophy*, p. 232, from the essay on 'The Decline and Fall of Causality' (Macmillan, London, 1968).

[2] Op. cit., p. 252.

events, in order to make its significant advance. At least, this ought to encourage theologians to engage in scientific determination of the specific kind of connection arising out of the realities into which they inquire, instead of being content to make use of the kind of connection which they find in operation elsewhere. It will not do for them, for example, simply to react against causal connection (*Ursache*) as developed by positivist science in favour of the kind of connection which Dilthey thought to be characteristic of the human sciences, namely, expression (*Ausdruck*), which has already led too many scholars and theologians up a blind alley. Quite clearly the sort of connection which theology requires must be more subtle and flexible, yet no less rational, than those traditionally isolated in the natural and human sciences, if it is to have the kind of precision and range appropriate to the interaction between God and the world, or divine and human agency, that belongs to the essential heart of its subject-matter. Here, I believe, theology can learn from another development in modern science, in the rise of *field theory*, that is, not from the material content of any particular field theory but from the way in which approach is made to the question of connection, from the actualities of the objective field.

The angle of our approach is quite determinative. If we approach nature by making primary the question as to concrete particularity, we inevitably dissect what we observe into discrete particles, which as such have then to be organized in a mechanical way, with all the limitations and problems that brings—which was, of course, the main approach of classical physics. But we get a rather different result when we make our primary question one as to the totality within which events, far from being isolated from one another in space and time, are already found in a field of continuous wave-like interconnections, where no single event can be apprehended adequately except in indissociable relationship with the whole. In the nature of the case, this kind of connection is not one that corresponds very easily with our observational representations, which tend to be discontinuous and particulate, but for that reason it is more objectively free from distortion through picturing or abstractive thought, and because the connection is one that derives from the active relations, transitions or processes in which events are already involved in space–time, it can be expressed appropriately only in dispositional language or differential equations of some sort or another.

In physics, for example, the field assumes the role provided in classical mechanics by the material points, and as determined by differential equations, it takes the place of force. It was in line with field-physics of this kind, which Einstein called 'probably the most profound transformation which has been experienced by the foundation of physics since Newton's time',[1] that relativity theory eventually developed. Yet it took a comparatively long time after the decisive work of James Clark Maxwell for physics to break free from the urge to interpret the field in mechanistic terms, before it could advance in the way it did with Einstein. Biology, on the other hand, has not yet found its Einstein or perhaps even its Maxwell. Although the direction in which it ought to travel has been pointed out by some of the greatest physicists and chemists of our day (such as Bohr and Polanyi), biology is still largely stuck in the attempt to interpret the field of living structures in mechanistic terms, and therefore in such a way that the distinctive kind of connection manifested in organisms is suppressed or reducted through explanation in terms of molecules alone, in accordance with the laws of physics and chemistry, to the kind of connection that obtains in some physical field (nuclear or perhaps electromagnetic). Nevertheless, even when great attempts are made to do justice to the special nature of this field it is extremely difficult not to distort or even to replace the relations naturally and functionally inherent in living structures with relations which we artificially develop by way of their reactions to our instruments for stimulation and observation. What seems to be needed is a renunciation of the old dichotomy between mechanism and vitalism and an axiomatic break-through by means of open premises into the inner logic of biological processes which will illuminate for us the distinctive character of connection in living systems. The great difficulty here, however, as W. M. Elsasser has recently pointed out, is that while organic matter is

[1] *Out of My Later Years*, p. 74.

characterized by great variability, complexity and inhomogeneity, we will try to construe it in terms of a logic of homogeneity. In other words, the distinctive kind of connection that is the property of living structures is so elusive to conceptualization through our traditional logic, that of homogeneous classes, that we require a logic of inhomogeneous classes in order to grasp and interpret it in accordance with what it actually is. Here then we have a situation in biological science comparable to that which physics has reached in the demand for quantum logic, and here too, as Elsasser goes on to show, we have to reckon with an irreducible logical complexity in which different levels of organization coupled together are required if we are to develop biological explanation and interpretation in an adequate way.

The aspect of field theory which it is most important for theology to note is that reality, hidden so far as our observations are concerned, is open to explanatory interpretation in essentially differential and functional relations, but we have to develop the kind of open axiomatic penetration that will reveal its natural logical structure. The kind of connection found in field theory can be so elastic and flexible that it requires on our part a new logic to cope with it. This is more difficult in biology than in physics, but it cannot be easier in theology where the distinctive connection is richer and more elusive, and ontological as well as dynamic. It must be conceived differentially in accordance with the divine and human poles of interaction, and therefore understood to be trans-historical as well as historical. This requires far more attention from theologians than they have given to it hitherto, for adequate explanatory interpretation must be developed ultimately from the side of the object and out of actual relations in the objective field, and not merely, as in much contemporary theology, from the side of the knowing subject.

3 A MORE ADEQUATE UNDERSTANDING OF CONCEPTUALITY

'In my opinion', Einstein once wrote, 'nothing can be said concerning the manner in which concepts are to be made and

---

[1] *Atom and Organism* (Princeton University Press, Princeton, 1966), pp. 14, 23ff., 31ff., 42ff., 57, 77ff., 128.

connected, and how we are to co-ordinate them to the experiences.'[1] Behind this lay the 'awe' and 'profound faith' which gripped him in face of the mystery of the world's comprehensibility and which he held to spring from the sphere of religion, but without which science would be blind.[2] In other words, although scientific knowledge is possible only on the assumption that nature is inherently intelligible, it is unable to adapt to logical fixation the relation between concepts and the realities with which they are co-ordinated, any more than we can reduce to statements alone the relation between statements and being, but that does not allow us to hold that the relation between scientific concepts and reality is non-conceptual or non-rational. Yet this is the view of a surprising number of people today, e.g. in a nominalist notion of science in which everything is ultimately resolvable into logical propositions, or in a romantic notion of religion in which faith is basically non-conceptual and theology without objective cognitive content. Both of these operate with a false dichotomy between conceptuality and reality. According to Einstein, however, scientific knowledge of the world rests upon a basis of 'primary concepts' (or 'fundamental relations') which are directly and intuitively connected with experience and derive their certainty through their applicability to it, while all other scientific concepts and notions are connected to this basis by means of theorems.[3] In this way our scientific knowledge in each field is co-ordinated rationally with the comprehensibility of the world. A 'dogmatic realism' of this kind (it is Einstein's expression) applies, I believe, *mutatis mutandis* of course, no less to theological science, and is even more to the point for here we are concerned with a profounder conceptual bond with being through the Word of God.

It is important to remember that, in the actual states from which we begin in any science, concepts are not found in isolation but are interlinked in a field of conceptuality which is co-ordinated with a continuous flow of orderly, intelligible happening in space and time. Our primary concepts arise in a situation where thought

---

[1] *Out of My Later Years*, p. 61.
[2] Ibid.
[3] Op. cit., p. 61ff.

is already and immediately engaged with reality which is the ontological basis and rational source of their development, and they function as the hermeneutic media through which reality is disclosed to us in its inner relations and we on our part are enabled to grasp it in accordance with its objective structure and interpret it to others through series of conceptual extensions. All concepts are properly defined by the conceptual field in which they function and ultimately have their meaning through the semantic co-ordination of that field with reality, but are immediately vague when they are detached or isolated.

Once again, then, it is through abstraction that our difficulties come upon us. When we detach concepts from their natural field of continuous interrelation in space-time and break them up into individuated clear-cut ideas, we snap their line of intelligible connection with reality, for it is through that field at its basic points that they are correlated with reality. Then we try to give them meaning by correlating them primarily with the knowing subject while a corresponding kind of organization must be found to give them coherence. But all this is to force through a deep-going division between subject and object, phenomenal things-for-us and noumenal things-in-themselves, meaning and reality, interpretation and fact, the conceptual and the non-conceptual. This is an impasse from which we cannot escape by trying to transcend the subject–object relation, or by flying from objective to take refuge in non-objective relations, for then we would only beat our heads against the prison walls of our own subjectivities.

All this, however, does serve to reveal a fundamental trait of our human concepts which must be taken seriously: their bi-polar structure through correlation with the subject as well as with the object. On the one hand, since we do not think alone but only with other minds, our concepts are rooted as interrelated forms of life in a socio-conceptual field, which means that in order to appreciate them we must probe into the psychological and social conditions underlying the shaping and organizing of our concepts. On the other hand, since we do not think without having intelligible objects of thought, our concepts are grounded in an objective field of orderly relations, which means that in order to understand them we must penetrate into the rational structure of the reality to which they refer and by which they are determined. Moreover, because our thought develops only through language and language exists only in society, we have to clarify the relation of our concepts in their objective content to the language of the society in which we live and speak, and of course to any language which we are using as the medium of our thought, communication or interpretation. Because it is through language that we are able to have a trans-subjective relation to being, language plays an enormous part in the objective reference of our concepts; but since language is moulded and shaped in the life and culture of society, it tends to hold our concepts captive to the traditional habits and prevailing use of language in society. This can easily give rise to a masterful conceptualization within the field of our organized subjectivities that is akin to objectifying thought and which tends to suppress or smother the objective reference of our concepts. Hence if science really is to clarify our thought and advance our knowledge of reality, it must make it one of its most persistent tasks to escape from the conservatism and recalcitrance of our ordinary habits of thought and speech.[1] This is one of the important places where a critical philosophy ought to be a great help to science, through analyses that break up the rigidity of language and open up our linguistic and conceptual schematisms to make room for new learning and thinking under the direct thrust of reality. Yet it is at this point that modern linguistic philosophy often appears so backward and useless to the scientist, for it seems to be tied down to the syntactical and sermocinal thinking carried in ordinary language and thus to be geared into the obsolescence of traditional verbalization.

In noting the relevance of these questions for theology, we may begin with the relation between concepts and language which is such a pressing issue today in view of the wide hiatus that has opened up between talk about God and talk about the world. The language of every society has grown up with its common life and culture and continues as the public medium in which its meaning

[1] See the important discussion of ordinary language by Waismann, *How I see Philosophy*, pp. 172ff.

is reflected and understandable communication takes place, but it is inevitably the deposit of modes of thought and turns of speech that function in dependence upon the ordinary subject–object and subject–subject structures that arise in the interrelations of people and things in this world. When we who dwell in this language and the conceptual habits immanent in it turn to what Karl Barth once called 'the strange new world within the Bible'[1] we have not a little difficulty in adjustment. We must translate what we learn into our ordinary language if it is to be understandable and communicable; but we learn nothing new unless we break out of the grooves in which our thought has already been directed to run through our ordinary language. This is where an alert theology has an all-important role to play, in constructive as well as critical activity, in demanding and carrying through a significant shift in the meaning of ordinary terms to cope with the new insights and in creating new forms of expression apposite to new truth where the adaptation of old forms of speech and thought does not prove adequate. Of course, every lively and advancing science must create new linguistic apparatus as well as new instruments and mechanisms for its investigations. Without the refinement of linguistic and cognitive tools we would be unable to grasp and give shape in our minds to genuinely new truth. Hence it is most important for us to resist the pressure of those popular theologians and linguistic philosophers who appear to have a superstitious veneration for ordinary language in their insistence that nothing is valid which is not describable within its compass. There is in fact, as Waismann insists, a rational element in dissatisfaction with existing language, 'the fight of thought with the obtuseness of speech', for 'the breaking away from the norm is often the only way of making oneself understand'.[2]

There is a further implication for theology here. Since we cannot escape using ordinary language in our attempts to make the truth plain to ourselves and others, our hard-won concepts inevitably participate in the socio-conceptual structures in which we live. They tend to get trapped in them and obscured by the way

---

[1] *The Word of God and the Word of Man* (1928), p. 28.
[2] *How I see Philosophy*, p. 201.

in which they condition and shape our expression of them. And so they end up by being unable to convey to us anything more than what we can tell ourselves through other notions. For this reason, the formulation of our concepts requires constant revision and the concepts themselves require constant reconstruction in the interest of purity of thought as well as advance in knowledge. This is done by keeping our concepts as close as possible to the objective source that gave rise to them, for that is the only way in which they can be renewed in their original force and rationality. This lets us see how far astray we go when we think theology can be renewed, commended and communicated to our contemporaries if only we can transpose it all into ordinary language.

We recall that human concepts have a bi-polar structure through correlation with the object and correlation with the subject. If this polarization of conceptuality gets broken up we are apt to fall into a false dichotomy between the conceptual and the non-conceptual, construing the latter as a non-knowing relation to the object, and placing the former entirely within the power of our active reason. Concepts thus become subjectively and not objectively defined; they are the rational shape we give to whatever we try to understand. If so, it is not surprising that we conclude that our concepts are incapable of grasping reality which transcends conceptuality altogether. At best such concepts only aim at reality; but if they are not correlated with its inherent intelligibility, they are no more than blind shots in the dark. This is the development, taking its rise from the radical dualism of post-Cartesian philosophy, which has worked itself out in Neo-Protestant thought into the kind of agnosticism that is so familiar to us today. It is thus rather strange to find the so-called 'new theology' in the Roman Church, under the influence of phenomenology, now travelling along this same path, as in reaction to the hard conceptualization of Scholastic theology it plays with the 'liberating' force of 'the non-conceptual element' in knowledge of God. If by this is meant an empirical as well as a conceptual relation to the object, the 'non-conceptual' meaning 'more than conceptual', it is understandable but still misleading, if what is conceptual is defined solely in terms of the grasping power of the active intellect and not also in terms of the intelligible self-evidence of the divine reality and the intuitive apprehension and intellectual consent which it compels in us. Once a gap between the conceptual and the non-conceptual has been posited in this way, it will not do to appeal to 'infused grace' which in a roundabout way is said to give objective and intelligible content to faith in spite of the alleged 'non-evidence' of the divine Being. Far from getting rid of the fatal dualism it derives from the Augustinian tradition, it reinforces it by interposing a 'supernatural' order between God and the created world.

What is required is a more adequate understanding of the polarization of conceptuality with its objective and its subjective reference, in which reality seizes our minds and sets up within them the law of its own rationality. True concepts thus have a transcendental aspect in that they arise in us through direct and intuitive apprehension of reality in its own evidence and objective hermeneutic force, but this is an implicit conceptuality which becomes explicit in our apprehension as we listen to it and let it become articulate and take shape within the rationality immanent in our human forms of thought and speech. Even so, our concepts refer to more than they can ever specify in explicit forms, for they are rooted in a reality which they cannot exhaust but that reaches out far beyond in an indefinite range of objectivity and intelligibility. In our knowledge of God conception takes place under the impact of His Word and Spirit. Through His Word God confronts us with the inner speech of His divine being and through His Spirit He evidences Himself to us in the presence of His reality, in such a way that He creates in us the capacity to hear, recognize and apprehend Him, and evokes from us the consent and understanding of faith in His self-revelation. Knowledge of God is thus conceptual in its essential root (*fides esse nequit sine conceptione*, as Anselm said),[1] with a conceptuality that derives from God's self-revelation in Word, but which we have to bring to articulate expression in our understanding, with a conceptuality that finds

---

[1] *De concordia*, q. iii. . . . . 'fides est ex hoc, quod concipit mens per auditum; neque ita ut sola conceptio mentis faciat fidem in homine, sed quia fides esse nequit sine conceptione.' (*Opera Omnia*, edit. by F. S. Schmitt, II, p. 271: 6-8).

shape in our human forms of thought and speech, yet under the control of God's own intelligible reality.

In answer to the question as to how both poles of this conceptuality are related, we may want to return to the view of Einstein that this is something which in the nature of the case we are unable to state and which we must be content to accept as part of the mystery of the comprehensibility of things. But it is at this point in the knowledge of God that we have to take into account the epistemological relevance of God's Spirit for an explanation of our knowledge from the side of the object and in accordance with its nature. That is something that will be taken up later, at some length, but meantime several considerations need to be added to this introductory discussion.

(a) Not a little help may be derived from the patristic distinction between *apprehending* and *comprehending*. In apprehending God we do not just grasp part of Him for He is one and indivisible, but this does not mean that we can bring the totality of God within the compass of our comprehension. Apprehension is a grasping of God which does not exhaust His transcendent reality and mystery; but it is no less conceptual for that reason, since it is the form of conception rationally appropriate to His divine nature and majesty. Hence it does not follow from the fact that we are unable to give a precise conceptual definition of the reality of God that it cannot be conceptually grasped but may only be envisaged in some indefinite, non-conceptual way. Conception of God involves a differential relation within it in accordance with the nature of the divine and of the human pole. We know God or rather, as St. Paul put it, are known of God. We know God only in that we are seized by His reality. It is in response to that divine grasping of us that our human grasping of Him takes place, in functional dependence upon Him, as an act of 'under-standing'. Hence the distinction to be drawn is not between non-conceptual and conceptual knowing of God, nor even between apophatic and cataphatic knowledge, but between *cataleptic* apprehending and cataphatic comprehending. Both are conceptual acts, but only the former is a grasping of God that is appropriate to His divine nature. In it the Word of God seizes our minds, sets up within their conceiving the force of its own rationality, and thus opens them to conceptual understanding of God.

(b) It is important to remember, as Frege has pointed out, that while a word may awaken for us some sort of picture (or representation), the picture does not need to correspond to its content, so that a word without any corresponding inner picture is not for that reason lacking in content or meaning.[1] Thus, when our thought leads us far beyond the imaginable, it need not thereby be deprived of a rational basis. Any denial of this would be equivalent to the identification of the conceivable with the picturable. This is similar to the point we noted earlier, that while we set up an experiment in nuclear physics in accordance with the kind of causal connection held to obtain in classical physics, this does not mean that this causality must apply to the new kind of connection that comes to light through the experiment, for it can be apprehended only on a different logical basis, with a renunciation of the criterion of perceptibility. Here the conceivable is precisely what does not correspond to the picturable, but is no less rational for that reason.

This holds good also for our knowledge of the invisible God, which must be expressed in human and creaturely forms of thought and speech. While there is no correspondence between the pictures latent in the language expressing our theological concepts and the realities to which we refer, this does not invalidate the concepts, for the conceptual relation they involve lies beyond the range of the imaginable. Indeed this is the only kind of conceptual relation that would be appropriate to God. A denial of this would surely involve a naive identification of the conceptual with the imaginable, or the genuinely objective with the objectifiable. Thus to claim that, since the creaturely and representational 'content' of our conceptions does not correspond to anything in the reality of God, we have to reckon in the last analysis with a non-conceptual relation to Him, would be a serious lapse from rationality. Behind such a claim, however, which is still being made by some Roman and Protestant theologians, there evidently lies a

[1] *The Foundations of Arithmetic*, §§ 59–60 (tr. by J. L. Austin, 2nd ed., Blackwell Oxford, 1953, p. 70f.).

rupture in the polarization of conceptuality, which posits such a conceptual gap that they cannot bring themselves to think that we can grasp and understand God conceptually. This is why the problem of the analogical relation in our knowledge of God is so crucial for them; but within the position they seem to have adopted it is extremely difficult, if not impossible, to find a solution to it, especially when it concerns detached and individuated concepts.

(c) In pointing out that a word can have meaning and content even if the mental picture it recalls for us has no connection with the object of our thought, Frege also insisted that we must not consider the words individually but look for their meaning in the sentence in which they are used. It is from the sentence as a whole that the words receive their content.[1] When we are concerned with concepts, however, we must look for their meaning in the field of conceptuality in which they are found to be functioning. The whole field is possessed of meaning in so far as it is co-ordinated with experience through certain primary concepts or relations which are intuitively and directly apprehended. The other concepts functioning in the field have their meaning through theorems connecting them with the primary concepts within the compass of the field, although they themselves do not have any correspondence with our experience. The theorems, however, which express the relations between the concepts do have at least an indirect relation to experience evident in their applicability to what is intuitively apprehended through the primary concepts. In this way, Einstein argued,[2] science develops a system of stratification between layers of concepts or relations which are co-ordinated in such a way as to enable us to penetrate through intermediate layers of a temporary nature down to the narrowest basis of fundamental concepts or relations through which we may reach the greatest conceivable unity in our understanding of the world. In other words, it is by operating with different levels of conceptuality that we are able to clarify the logic of the conceptual fields and determine the fundamental concepts which, through

---

[1] Op. cit. § 60 (p. 70).
[2] *Out of My Later Years*, pp. 62ff.

their objective bond with reality, form the basis for the illumination and organization of all our knowledge in that field.

Viewed in this light, the whole question of the analogical relation in our knowledge of God becomes at once simpler and profounder through the co-ordination of conceptual levels by reference to which the individual concepts are defined. Thus we are not concerned how to specify direct analogical correspondence between the father–son concept or relation which derives from our human experience and the Father–Son relation in God. That would bring in its train all the problems fabricated by the detachment and isolation of concepts which we have discussed above. The analogical relation between them can be determined only in a co-ordination of whole levels of conceptual relations with one another and through the ultimate co-ordination of their basic concepts with intelligible relations in God. In this way we discover that the Father–Son relation in God is not to be construed simply as an extension of the father–son relation in our human experience, and that we are able to think of God conceptually in this way, without demanding that relations in God correspond to the picture latent in our human language as to fatherhood and sonship, because the eloquent self-evidence of God in His Word takes cataleptic control of our conceiving of Him, with the result that our use of 'Father' and 'Son' to speak of God is not merely a projection toward Him but a conception controlled by what God is in Himself. It is indeed, as St. Paul said, from the Fatherhood of God that all other fatherhood derives its meaning. However, the clarification of our basic concepts this understanding requires and the penetration into their fundamental unity, with all the disclosure of objectivity and enlightenment that brings, involves the development of theology as a *dogmatic science* in the strict and proper sense.

II THEOLOGY OLD AND NEW

2

The Eclipse of God [1]

Under this title I would like to speak about certain epistemological issues that appear to lie behind a good deal of modern thought. I have taken the title itself from a remarkable little book by Martin Buber which arose out of lectures given in several American Universities in 1951, in which he diagnosed some of the basic problems that have since come out into the open, not only in the so-called 'new theology' of John Robinson, Harry Williams, Paul Van Buren or Werner Pelz, but in the 'God is dead' theology of Thomas Altizer and William Hamilton. An eclipse of the sun, Buber reminds us, is something that occurs between the sun and our eyes, not in the sun itself. So it is with the eclipse of God that is now taking place, for something has stepped between our existence and God to shut off the light of heaven, but that something is in fact *ourselves*, our own bloated selfhood. The root problem of the 'new theologians' would seem to lie in the fact that they are unable to distinguish God from their own swollen subjectivity.

Let us begin by trying to get our historical bearings, so that we can plot some of the changes that have been taking place.

There have been three periods of vast cosmological change in our western history. The first of these took place between the second and fourth centuries when our outlook upon the world underwent a considerable mutation, that is from the primitive cosmology of the Greeks to what came to be known as Ptolemaic cosmology in which a new astronomical system was elaborated in conjunction with a theory of radical disjunction between the

[1] Reprinted from *The Baptist Quarterly*, Vol. XXII, No. 4, Oct. 1967, pp. 194–214.

heavenly and the earthly realms. A vast shift in outlook took place to which there corresponded an equally great shift in meaning and in the reference of statements. In such a period of profound mutation the really basic epistemological questions come to the surface and decisions have to be taken.

This was the period of controversy and strife in the history of the Church. It emerged with the problems of Gnosticism and moved through Arianism to the great Christological debates when the fundamental grammar of the Christian faith had to be set out and knowledge of God in the revelation of Jesus Christ had to be secured. During these centuries of change there was a great deal of confusion in which one-sided interpretations of the Christian faith arose which attempted to entrench themselves in the Church through their appeal to the popular mind, but which turned out to be dangerous rationalizations in theological form of sub-Christian religion. Thus the period in which Gnosticism and Arianism were rampant proved to be an interim stage of change in which people had not yet discerned the real implications of the Christian Gospel, but the Christian Church passed through those ages of struggle with heresy and emerged with its faith more firmly rooted and more rationally apprehended.

The second great mutation in cosmological outlook seems to have begun in the fourteenth century and to have reached its zenith in the seventeenth century, although from our point of view it is what took place in the sixteenth century that is particularly important. This was the change from the Ptolemaic cosmology to the post-Copernican or Newtonian cosmology. Once again, the basic problems of knowledge emerged in the open, the same fundamental questions were raised, and a similar period of confusion, misunderstanding and error is to be found, immediately before and after the Reformation. But when the Church came through it, Christian faith was again more firmly established and more profoundly understood.

Today we are in the midst of the third great mutation in thought, in the change from a Newtonian to a post-Einsteinian cosmology, from classical physics to nuclear physics. Once again a vast shift in meaning and fundamental understanding is taking place in which the slant of our concepts and the reference of our statements are being affected. Today too we have the same sort of confusion that we find in the two earlier periods, although in many ways it is more like the first than the second. The real issues are basically the same as in the third and fourth centuries, while we have the same kind of popular theology that in Gnosticism and Arianism gripped the imagination of the popular mind but menaced the foundations of the Christian Church through a subtle form of atheism. This is the soil in which the 'new theology' has sprung up, but it must be regarded as a symptom of change and confusion that will pass, for we shall find our faith more adequately grounded and our apprehension of God in Christ more clear and rational than before.

Our problems, of course, have a very different setting from those in the Early Church, for they go back to the great change that took place during the Reformation and are cast in a very different idiom and style of thought. In order to get at our problems from behind, as it were, let me discuss four major changes in thought that took place during the Reformation and have affected us all in the modern world, although I shall speak of them for the most part as they appear in the contribution of John Calvin, because it is that aspect of them that I know best.

(1) At the very beginning of his *Institute of the Christian Religion* Calvin made it clear that there is a mutual relation between the knowledge of God and the knowledge of ourselves. That can be taken to mark the beginning of modern theology, for it is within this orbit that all our theological thinking since has moved. We do not know God in the abstract as He is in Himself, but only in the reciprocal relation which He has established through His revelation between God and us and us and God. The only God we know is the God who has made Himself known, the God of whom we human beings have experience, so that in the nature of the case we cannot construct a knowledge of God outside this God-man or man-God relationship. We know Him only as we ourselves are affected by that knowledge and acquire a deeper knowledge of ourselves before Him, so that there is inevitably a human coefficient in all *our* knowledge of God. For Calvin this

involved also an acutely personal relation with God, for God addresses us personally in His Word and summons us to make a personal response in obedient love, and it is out of that obedience to God's self-revelation that our knowledge grows and deepens. Yet Calvin also insisted that while God's self-revelation demands of us personal reciprocity, nevertheless within this mutuality the emphasis is laid decidedly upon the objective pole of the relationship. We know God truly only as we are cast upon His own transcendent reality and as we think out of a centre in that reality and not out of a centre in ourselves. While we cannot know Him without knowing ourselves, we know Him truly only as we are able to distinguish Him in the dignity and majesty of His own Truth from ourselves.

Thus at the same time there took place in the Reformation a considerable change in understanding of the nature of truth, which we may speak of as a change from *cognitive truth* to the *truth of being*. This is extremely important, while it is highly instructive to see that the change came about along with the recovery of the place of the human subject in the knowledge of God. There cannot be any doubt that the great realist thought of St. Thomas Aquinas was concerned with the truth of being, but when it was defined in terms of intellectual apprehensibility as the adequation between reality and mind the emphasis was inevitably laid upon cognitive truth. It was thus that medieval theology became engrossed with abstractive knowledge, theology in which truth and statement, being and concept, are bound up so closely together that they cannot be separated from each other. Medieval thought was always trying to bridge the gap between thought and being by thought alone, so that its theology and its science became abstract and rationalist.

The theology of Calvin represents a radical revolt from this way of thinking. The Truth is God Himself in His own Being, God incarnate in Jesus Christ, not our statements about God, and not even Biblical statements about Him. They may be true but their truth resides in God and not in themselves. Their truth resides in Christ and not in us. Therefore, when we really know God and speak about Him in His self-giving to us in Christ we are

emancipated from ourselves and our own speaking. We are made
free and open for God and are cast upon the sheer Truth of the
divine Being and His active self-revelation. Hence in testing our
knowledge of God and our speech about Him we must let
ourselves be called into question lest we confound the Truth of
God with our forms of thought and speech about it.

(2) The next great change we note in Calvin's thought is a
change in scientific questioning. Aristotle had posited four fundamental questions in all scientific knowledge, but by medieval
times these had been reduced to three, *quid sit*, *an sit*, and *quale sit*,
asked in that order. *Quid sit* is the question as to the 'what' or the
essence of a thing; *an sit* is the question as to the 'how' or the
possibility of a thing; while *quale sit* is the question as to the actual
nature and character of a thing. Asked in that order, they were
questions that began with abstraction and possibility and then went
on to actuality. But Calvin reversed the order of these questions
and began with the last of them, *quale sit*, preferring to ask first
of all, What is the actual nature of this thing that we know? In
this way he allowed the nature of what we know to determine
how we actually know it, without laying down any conception
of it or prescribing how it must be known, apart from actual
knowledge of it. Put first in this way, *quale sit* becomes the primary question of modern science, 'What have we here?' while
the other questions when made to follow it become not abstract
questions as to essence and possibility but testing and controlling
questions designed to make sure that our actual knowledge rests
properly upon the ground that is claimed for it. Of course, the
question *quale sit* when directed to a personal reality becomes
qualis sit, that is, the question as to the 'who'. Thus, in Christian
theology the primary question becomes the question as to who
God is in the actual knowledge of Him in which we are involved
in the Church, followed by the other questions probing into the
ground of this knowledge to make sure that it really does derive
from God and repose upon Him as its given reality.

This is the way in which modern science has developed its
questioning in sharp contrast to medieval and ancient science
which started off with the abstract questions as to the quiddities

and possibilities of things. But with the new method, scientific questioning is liberated from philosophical preconceptions, and knowledge can be pursued empirically under the determination of the nature of what we seek to know, in progressive emancipation from extraneous assumptions. Thus we seek to know things as far as possible out of themselves, unobstructed by external authorities or metaphysical prejudices or alien dogmatisms. So far as Reformation theology was concerned, this meant a mode of theological inquiry in which we seek to know God more and more out of His own self-revealing Word, and not from the presuppositions lodged in the authoritative tradition of the Church, and so far as modern science was concerned this meant a mode of inquiry in which we break free from the situation in which final causes have been clamped down upon nature, in order to let nature disclose itself freely to us in untrammelled empirical inquiry.

At the same time there took place, and this is particularly clear in the work of Calvin, a radical change in the nature of the *question* itself. In Latin this represents a change from *quaestio* to *interrogatio*. *Quaestio* is the kind of question you ask in solving a problem in knowledge you already have, in order to move from confusion to clarity. Questions of this kind arise in a complex of relations of ideas where the answer is to be found by straightening out the logical connections. That was the kind of question pursued in medieval science, so that in medieval times a scientific theology had to be cast in the rigorous form of *quaestiones*. Problematic thinking of this kind has certainly an important and necessary place, but Calvin felt the kind of question it involves is not primary and is not finally a genuine question at all. A genuine question is one in which you interrogate something in order to let it disclose itself to you and so reveal to you what you do not and cannot know otherwise. It is the kind of question you ask in order to learn something *new*, which you cannot know by inferring it from what you already know.

It is interesting to note that this change in questioning took place first in the study of law and in the logic of 'question and answer' that developed in the interrogation of documents and witnesses; it was then transferred into theology, e.g. by Calvin, and transferred again from law and theology into natural science, e.g. by Francis Bacon. Both Calvin and Bacon, of course, had been trained in the new Renaissance approach to law, Bacon being also influenced by Calvin. But it came into law through the work of Laurentius Valla, who had studied the ancient lawyers, Cicero above all, and applied their method of interrogation to the scrutiny of historical documents including the Scriptures and even sought to develop a method of 'logical discovery'. This was the notion of *interrogation* that Calvin applied to the Holy Scriptures and to theology. We have to ask genuine questions of God in order to let Him disclose Himself to us. Theology is not the systematic manipulation of ideas we already have or find in the Church or the working of them up into problems which we set ourselves to answer. In proper theological inquiry we ask open questions in order to allow God to answer us, and to give us answers which we do not already know but which, in so far as they are really new, cut across what we already think we know. It was this kind of inquiry, *activa inquisitio*, that Calvin also applied to Biblical interpretation, that Bacon applied to the interpretation of 'the books of nature', and then from Bacon it was applied back, although in a more rationalist manner, by Benedict Spinoza to the interpretation of the sacred Scriptures.

It is scientific questioning of this kind that has dominated the whole of the modern world, but right from the start Reformation theology and empirical science interacted in its development. Of course, the mode of questioning and the nature of the question go together, in accordance with the nature of that into which inquiry is being made, so that scientifically the kind of question and the way in which it is put will vary in accordance with the nature of the field of inquiry. In order to know God we do not 'torment' Him as we do nature before it will disclose its secrets to us, but it nevertheless remains true that active interrogation and modern reformed theology belong together.

(3) The third main change that I wish to note is rather more subtle and difficult, although it can be stated in quite a simple form. It is about the relation of language to being and of signs

to things signified, and the transition from the medieval to a modern way of thinking about this that concerns us.

Let me put the problem in this way. You cannot state in statements how statements are related to being: otherwise you convert the relation of statements to being into mere statements. To use Wittgensteinian language, you cannot picture in a picture how a picture pictures some reality, because if you did everything would become picture, with no reality. From one point of view, this was the persistent problem of medieval thought. If you think you can reduce to statements how statements are related to the Truth of God you have resolved everything without remainder into statements alone. As I understand it, it is the same problem that is to be found both in medieval realism and in medieval nominalism, and it is at this point that they tended to pass over into each other, in the identification of statement with the truth. It is essentially the same difficulty that lies in the heart of rationalist fundamentalism, the identification of truth with statement about it. Let me put the matter in still another way that is taken from Plato in his discussion of the relation of the words or 'names' to the realities they signify. If you think of words as somehow 'imaging' realities, as the Greeks tended to do, then the more exact words are the more closely they imitate what they signify; but when the image is a perfect replica of the reality it signifies, how can you distinguish them? The image will inevitably tend to replace the reality in your thought. Similarly words come to act as substitutes for things and to oust them as the objects of our thought, so that we think words and statements and not things through them—this is especially easy where the 'things' are invisible realities, and is therefore a particular danger for theology.

The relation between language and being that lies behind this began to come under severe attack before the Reformation, so that some new understanding had to develop. It came out of the notion of *intention*. When you make a statement you intend to refer to something of which you have some experience or idea in yourself. Here you have a subjective pole, the mind of the speaker, and an objective pole, the thing referred to. According to William of Occam, we are more sure of the state of our own mind or soul than of the external existent or referent, that is, of what he called the *oblique intention* rather than the *direct intention*. Roughly speaking, two different views diverged from this point, for which we can let Erasmus and Calvin stand as our representatives. What do we do when we interpret the Holy Scripture? How do we regard the relation between the words and the things they signify?

In answer to these questions, Erasmus took up Occam's doctrine of intention but gave it a more psychological and ethical turn. He interpreted biblical writers by penetrating into the subjective pole of their intention, that is, into their states of soul, and by reading what they wrote as expressions of their inner experiences. For Erasmus this meant to a large extent an interpretation of traditional biblical and theological teaching in terms of moral inwardness. Thus there began what has come to be known as 'modernism', a reinterpretation of Christianity through redacting its direct statements about God and His saving acts in our world into statements expressing inward moral states or attitudes of soul.

Calvin, like Luther, took the opposite point of view in which he sought to interpret the Scriptures mainly in accordance with their direct intention, that is by following the intention of the biblical writers through to the realities they intended their statements to refer to. The principle that Calvin followed here is taken from Hilary of Poitiers who laid it down that we must not subordinate things to the words that indicate them but the words to the things they indicate, for it is of the things themselves that we think rather than the words used of them. This is particularly important, as Hilary insisted, when we come to speak of God, for we cannot describe Him in language or reduce His Truth to statements. Theological language is indicative, not descriptive, of God and it is to be understood only as we allow it to refer us beyond itself to God in His transcendent reality. It was by developing this view of the relation of language to being that Calvin became the father of modern biblical interpretation.

These two very different approaches can be characterized briefly by asking what we do when we interpret St. Mark's Gospel. Do we seek to find out what was going on in the soul of Mark and interpret what he has to say as an outward expression of his inward moral and spiritual attitudes? Or do we interpret him in accordance with his direct intention to bear witness to Jesus Christ and a series of historical events in which God Himself was interacting with human existence? Are we to go behind what Mark is actually saying to offer some oblique interpretation of his literary work or are we to allow Mark to direct us to Jesus Christ in such a way that the language that is used is subordinated to Jesus Christ Himself? In the former case, our criterion for interpreting Mark's use of language can only be our own moral condition, but in the latter we must judge the adequacy of Mark's language in the light of the Reality to which it bears witness.

This distinction corresponds closely to that drawn by I. A. Richards many years ago in his *Principles of Literary Criticism* between two uses of language, an *emotive* and a *scientific* use of language. In the former we use language for the sake of the effects, emotions or attitudes that it produces, which is characteristic of poetry, but in the latter we use language for the sake of the reference, true or false, which it promotes, which is characteristic of science. Of course we can never eliminate the first, for language after all is a symbolic medium of communication in which the subjective pole of human intention has an essential part to play. But we use language scientifically only when the primary intention is brought into play and its deliberate reference is taken seriously. We cannot eliminate the fact that St. Mark put something of himself into his witness and into his writing, yet his primary intention was to speak not of himself but of Jesus Christ. If we are to deal faithfully with St. Mark, we must look at the reality to which he points and interpret what he has to say primarily in the light of it—otherwise we fall down badly in regard to basic scientific procedure.

(4) We have still to consider something quite fundamental, a change in the doctrine of God and His relation to nature. In the medieval theology it was very difficult to separate God from nature, for the knowledge of God and of the world were posited together. If we begin with nature and try to reach knowledge of God as the First Cause through a consideration of His effects in the world of created realities, we are unable to rise above those

realities but can only construe God as necessarily related to them. If we begin with God as the eternal and changeless One and then think of all created realities as the objects of His eternal knowing and willing, then we develop a notion of nature as eternally co-existing with God or at least in His Mind. God and nature were correlative concepts, as it were, but this had a very damaging effect upon 'nature' because it gave it a changeless character through a timeless relation to the divine causation—nature was in its heart impregnated with divine causes.

Deep in the Middle Ages, however, mainly through Duns Scotus, there emerged again the doctrine of creation out of nothing, in which God was thought of as creating the world by producing new ideas through which the world was given form and order as well as being. But it was with the Reformation that there was revived the biblical idea of God who creates the world out of nothing as something entirely distinct from Himself while yet dependent upon Him for its being and order. This at once emancipated the study of nature from philosophical preconceptions and led to the disenchantment of nature of its secret divinity. Men realized that they could understand nature only by looking at nature and not by looking at God. God means us to examine nature in itself, to learn about it out of itself, and not from the study of the Holy Scriptures or of theology. But it was the clear and unambiguous doctrine of God as the Creator of nature out of nothing that emancipated nature in this way for the investigations of empirical science. We know God by looking at God, by attending to the steps He has taken in manifesting Himself to us and thinking of Him in accordance with His divine nature. But we know the world by looking at the world, by attending to the ways in which it becomes disclosed to us out of itself, and thinking of it in accordance with its creaturely nature. Thus scientific method began to take shape both in the field of natural science and in the field of divine science.

When we consider all these four points of change and set them together we can see how revolutionary was the mutation of thought that occurred at the Reformation and what an enormous advance the Western world took at that time in theology as in natural science, but we can also see how closely theology and natural science interacted in their development into modern times. What happened, then, to these four major points and what is happening to them in the world in which we live today? Let us consider them one by one.

(1) It was the first that constituted the biggest problem, for it has worried us ever since. You cannot have a knowledge of God cut off from the fact that you know Him, but nor can you know anything cut off from the fact that you know it: the human subject has an ineradicable place in knowledge. The object of knowledge is always relative to a subject. How then can we get really objective knowledge unaffected by the human observer or thinker? So far as theology is concerned, history has often taken the way of Erasmus rather than the way of Calvin—it was Erasmus, you remember, who first pointed out that when you study history you are really studying yourself. You see, in the polar relation of our human knowledge, it is the subjective pole that tends to get more and more masterful so that the human subject, the self, gets in the way of the object he is studying. Granted that all theology is personal, involves a personal relation between you and God, must this be pursued in such a way that you get in between yourself and God so that you cannot see God beyond yourself? In the book I mentioned earlier Martin Buber insists that when we interpret encounters with God as self-encounters, man's very structure is destroyed—and that, he says, is the portent of the present hour.

This is the problem with Gogarten who interprets history as a form of self-encounter, for history is what we men create; and this is the problem with Bultmann who argues that when we speak about God the only content our statements can have is the determination of our existence by the impact of His 'Word' upon us, and so he reduces the content of revelation to our own 'self-understanding'. But is this not also a basic problem with John Robinson, that he is a theological solipsist, who cannot see finally outside of himself or identify a God 'out there' in distinction from the ground of his own being, and who makes matters much worse by insisting on thinking of God only 'in pictorial images' for then he is unable even to conceive of a theism except in the obsolete forms of a Ptolemaic cosmology? Is it not Dr. Robinson himself who requires, as it were, to be demythologized? But we are concerned here with a far deeper problem than that of a few notorious thinkers out on the flanks of historic Christianity: it is the problem of an ingrowing subjectivity, a sort of stuck-adolescence, that has come to effect multitudes of modern people, who are unable to break out of the teenage mentality in which they are engrossed with their own self-fulfilment, and are unable to reach the maturity of those who love their neighbours object-ively for their own sakes, because they cannot love God objec-tively for His sake. Their relations with God and with their neigh-bour are inverted upon themselves. Scientifically speaking, this is the loss of objectivity, a failure to understand things out of them-selves in accordance with their natures. That is why we have to regard not a little of the 'new theology' as an irrational flight from the exact thinking of science.

(2) What has happened to the change in the nature and mode of scientific questioning? In pure science itself steady headway continues to be made in the direction pointed out by Calvin and Bacon, but serious problems have arisen here also. When Bacon spoke about putting nature to the question and even tormenting it in order to force it to yield its secrets, he also insisted that tor-mented nature is still nature and that men inquiring into nature are part of nature, so that we can never get beyond nature; but he insisted above all that in order to know nature we must cast away from us the masterful idols of the mind, our prefabricated conceptions, and seek to interpret nature humbly as its servant. This is certainly the way to dominion over the earth, for its gives us power, technical power, but we may enter into this kingdom only like little children, following the ways nature herself lays down for us. But when this idea of putting nature to the question was taken up by Kant a change began to set in. Nature after all is dumb; she cannot talk back to us. Hence we must not only frame the questions we put to nature but also put into the mouth of nature the answers she is to give back to us. Indeed, in prescribing the kind of question we put to nature, we prescribe and preform

the kind of answers we get back from her. What this means then, it is sometimes argued, is that by our stipulations we impose our own pattern and mind upon nature; the only nature we know is the nature that is formed and shaped in our understanding of it.

Astonishing as it may seem, there are lots of people today who really believe this, who think, for example, that mathematics is a pure invention of the mind for it is not something forced upon us by the inherent nature of things, or who think that in the last resort science is about propositions, not about realities in the world 'out there' independent of us. But let us look at it quite simply. When a scientist lays bare the anatomical and physiological structure of the human body, he is not creating and imposing patterns upon it. When you yourself observe crystalline formations in the rocks you are not importing into them geometrical patterns of your own inventing, you think the geometrical patterns you find embedded in them already. That is why our basic statements are formed by way of conceptual assent to what is there or by way of recognition of an intelligibility inherent in the nature of things. This is certainly the astonishing thing that keeps on striking the scientist with wonder and awe, as Einstein used to say, that there is already embedded in nature an inherent rationality which it is the task of science to bring to light and express. Apart from it there could be no science at all. Thus the mathematical equations and even the new geometries we construct are quite meaningless unless they are applicable to nature, but if they are applicable to nature they are elaborated expressions of an objective rationality lying in nature itself. Of course, our difficulty in all knowledge, in physics and even in pure mathematics, is to make sure that subjective elements do not obtrude into our theories and obscure and distort our knowledge, and so it is a necessary part of science that we devise methods of reaching and expressing knowledge of something in such a way that our understanding of it is really subordinated to the nature and rationality of the thing itself. But even this stringent self-correcting scientific method is only a rigorous extension of the basic rationality we employ in every act of right knowledge.

It is in the realm of microphysics, however, that we come up against our biggest difficulties, for there, it is claimed, we are engaged in operations of measurement and 'observation' which include the human subject in the theoretic constructions in such a way that there is an impassable gulf between the subject and the objective reality. And this, it is argued, means the collapse of the whole structure of scientific objectivity, and that the way into the future must be one in which we learn to transcend the subject–object relation altogether. This panic conclusion shatters itself upon one simple fact, that we are never concerned in any science, and certainly not in microphysics any more than in chemistry, with objects that are only relative to subjects, but with objects that are also relative to other objects. It is in that interrelatedness of objects to one another that we find means of controlling our own subjectivities over against them and of distinguishing what is objectively real from our own subjective projections. What is happening, however, is that the idealist presuppositions latent in much of our thinking are being forced out into the open where we least expected to find them, in the realm of pure physics, but this has served to clear the air, for now nuclear physicists and mathematicians are at work in different parts of the world working out the objective nature of our knowledge in the microphysical realms in ways that do full justice to the fact that the discoveries in these areas of existence are not inventions of our minds but correspond to the nature of things, even though we are unable to describe them but can only produce cognitive instruments through which they come to be known. This means that modern science is moving on a massive front away from any transcending of the subject–object relationship into a profounder and a more massively grounded objectivity.

There is a remarkable parallel here between the difficulties of modern natural science and those of modern theology, for both are faced with the inordinate claims of human subjectivity in their own realms, and are struggling for the purity and genuineness of knowledge against the assertion that we can know only what we invent and fashion for ourselves. Let me put the problem quite sharply by pointing to the immense tension that exists in the universities between 'pure science' and 'technology'. By 'pure science' is meant here the kind of knowledge we reach in any field when we know realities out of themselves and in accordance with their own interior principles and not in terms of external authorities or imposed patterns of thought. This is what was called 'dogmatic science' in the seventeenth and eighteenth centuries, a term that was applied to physics before it was applied to theology. By 'technology' is meant here, not applied science, but the way of knowing by inventing in which we are more concerned to use nature than to know it, and claim to know only what we can create, and accept as true only what bears the imprint of our own minds. It is a similar kind of tension that we find in theology today, between 'pure theology' and 'new theology', between knowledge that is objectively determined by the nature of God in His self-revelation, and knowledge which we develop out of our own formative thought and expression. Think again of John Robinson in this connection. He is not a technologist but he is something of an artist in theology. He is not a scientific thinker who proceeds only by disciplined submission of his mind to the nature of things, but one who thinks in pictures and symbolic forms and imposes them upon reality, accepting them as valid in so far as they serve the purpose he has in mind. What is at stake here is the objectivity and genuineness of knowledge in which we distinguish what we know from our knowing it. Again and again in recent years I have found scientists who insist that in the tension between pure science and the new technology they share with us the same basic problem that faces us between pure theology and the 'new theology'. I am sure they are right. This is not to say, of course, that there is no room for technology in the proper sense as applied science, or for creative artistry in the realm of religion, but to insist that what is at stake here is the fundamental basis of rational knowledge.

(3) We turn now to the problems in the relation between language and being, and here we find ourselves engaged today in a set of linguistic and logical questions very like those that engaged some of the sharpest minds in the fourteenth, fifteenth and six-teenth centuries—which we cannot go into here. Of special importance in our own day is the distinction drawn long ago by Butler and Hume between relations of things or matters of fact

and relations of ideas. Scientific language is concerned basically with reference to matters of fact, but it is also and inevitably concerned with the relations of ideas if only because scientific statements must be brought into a truthful coherence with one another in order to do their job properly. Since scientific statements refer to realities beyond themselves they are not susceptible of 'demonstrative reasoning' in ideas alone, but they do offer compelling proof of their own by bringing our minds under the compulsion of the realities they 'map out'. Thus whenever a cluster of statements refers to a reality in such a way that there is disclosed an objective rationality in things that far outruns what can be specified of it at the moment and so manifests an indefinite range of enlightenment within which other problems and difficulties come to be simplified and solved, we are convinced that we have a true theory. This is the way that Michael Polanyi has taught us to understand the verifying processes of scientific thought and formulation.

It is essentially a similar movement of thought that engages us in theology, although here we are up against a different kind of rationality, not *Number* but *Logos*. But if in the scientific investigation of the world we consider that our thought has made contact with the real nature of things when we can bring our knowledge to a consistent and enlightening mathematical representation through which the inherent rationality of the world imposes itself upon us, so in scientific inquiry into the ways and works of God we consider that our thought has made genuine contact with the divine Reality when we can bring our knowledge to an intelligible and enlightening unity through which the *Logos* of God Himself presses itself convincingly upon our minds. We direct our questions to the self-giving of God in Jesus Christ and allow our minds to fall under the power of the divine rationality that becomes revealed in Him. It is a rationality inherent in the reality of the incarnate Word before it takes shape in our apprehension of it, but as we allow it to become disclosed to us under our questions and find that it is opened out before us in an objective depth that far transcends what we can specify of it in our formulations and yet is infinitely fertile in its illuminating power, we become caught up in a compulsive affirmation of it that is rational through and through. This is what we mean by scientific *theological* thinking, from an objective centre in the givenness of God, rather than popular *mythological* thinking, from a subjective centre in ourselves, in which we project our fabricated patterns and ideas upon the divine Reality and will accept only what we can conceive in terms of what we already know or what fits in with our own prior self-understanding.

It is not easy to disengage scientific thinking from popular thinking in any field of knowledge. This becomes evident, as Thomas Kuhn has shown us once again, whenever we are engaged in making some notable scientific advance, for the struggle to break free from preconceptions reveals how deeply conditioned even our scientific concepts can be by psychological and sociological factors at work in the community in which we live and work, or, following Frege, to put it the other way round, how easy it is for scientific achievements and discoveries to be corroded or even lost through the obtrusion into them of popular notions and mental pictures with which our ordinary language in any cultural context is impregnated. How frequently it is the half-baked scientist or the cheap popularizer who does irreparable damage to the onward advance of objective, scientific work. This is one of the most insidious problems we have to face in modern theology, where 'pop-theologians' compete with one another in the clamour for demotic adulation and notoriety.

Let us reflect a little more about the relation of language to culture which is so important to us all if only because of the enjoyment we derive from the great artistic and symbolic creations in literature. Good science or good theology will never disparage cultural development for they are part of it with much to contribute to it as well as much to learn from it. This is what makes so objectionable the new formalism initiated by James Barr in his strange disjunction of language from culture, evident, for example, in his denigration of von Humboldt. But it is the other extreme that concerns us here in which language is treated almost entirely as the self-expression of the soul or of the community and therefore as the precipitate of cultural development. Now when

religious language is regarded and interpreted in this way, theological statements become filled with a content taken from
contemporary culture. Then when we reach one of those critical
junctures in human history, such as the First World War, when
historic Christianity and the prevailing national culture are forced
apart, theological statements appear to a great many people to be
empty of real content, and they begin to wonder what has become
of 'God'. After the crisis, desperate attempts may be made to
reintegrate Christianity and culture, such as we see in Germany
after both world wars, if only to heal the traumatic rift in ethnic
consciousness. And so language about God is substantiated from
the consciousness of the community and its cultural creations. But
matters cannot rest there, for the more rapidly our culture advances the sharper the contrast between the one Christian Gospel
which is the same for all ages and nations and our contemporary
situation. Either historic Christianity must be completely re-
modelled as the religious expression of our culture or the cry goes
up that 'God is dead', for theological statements cannot be given
a 'meaning' in terms of the community's self-fulfilment. Then a
show-down is inevitable and the Christian Church finds itself
again in a missionary situation.

Theologically, the basic problem here is that language about
God has beome detached from the Reality of God, and a conceptuality arising out of our own consciousness has been substituted for
a conceptuality forced upon us from the side of God Himself. This
is the disaster which Martin Buber, to refer to the book already
mentioned once more, has called 'the conceptual letting go of God'.
Let us take our example of this from Paul Tillich, who has declared in a number of his works that faith-knowledge is symbolic
and non-conceptual so that if we are to pursue theology we must
borrow conceptualities from philosophy or science in order to
rationalize faith. That is to say, ultimately Tillich worked with a
romantic, non-conceptual approach to God. The rationality with
which he was concerned in his theology had become detached
from God, for he took it from his cultural involvement. Tillich
played a very important part in providing the rapid development
of religion in the United States after the Second World War with

a rational structure and respectability, but the way in which he did it involves him in some responsibility for the 'God is dead' way of thinking taken up by the small men. If the question as to God is correlated with the question as to man, and the question that man puts to God is finally himself, the questioner, it is difficult to see how the way of 'God' can avoid the way taken by man. And so the question as to God has become very acute in the United States as the Christian Church and American culture have tended to draw apart over the segregation issue. Whenever people prefer to follow a certain cultural way of life rather than the way of the Gospel that detaches us from our naturalistic existence, it is not surprising that they should find language about God rather empty and meaningless. All this lets us see how necessary a scientific theology is for the on-going life and mission of the Christian Church, for theology of this kind is the disciplined repentance to which the Church must constantly submit if its mind is not to be schematized to the patterns of this world but is to be renewed and transformed and grounded in the objective rationality of God in Jesus Christ.

(4) What happened to the change in the doctrine of God and nature that took place in the sixteenth century? As we saw, the old Stoic–Latin conception of God as *Deus sive natura* gave place to a more dynamic conception of Him as the living Creator actively at work in the world He has made. Nature was regarded as created out of nothing, utterly distinct from God but utterly dependent on Him for its being and order. Men learned to think differently of the world, in terms of its contingency and creatureliness, and learned to know it out of its natural processes. But more and more as men began to understand nature out of nature, they detached it from their thought of God and His creative activity, and regarded it as an independent source of knowledge and as the sphere of man's own creative activity. But as soon as nature was cut adrift in this way, there opened out an ever-widening gulf between God and the world, and an extensive process of secularization set in that affected the whole life and thought of man.

This means that the doctrine of God has moved from one extreme to the other, from such a juxtaposition of God and nature that one cannot be thought without the other, to such a complete disjunction between God and nature that God's activity is banished from the world He has made and nature is sealed off from any meaning beyond itself in God.

This cannot but have disastrous consequences for Christian theology for it cuts away from it any thought of the interaction of God with the world so that it makes impossible not only a doctrine of providence but any doctrine of incarnation, and it cuts away likewise any interaction between the revealing and saving activity of God and human historical existence so that God is made dumb, no real Word from Him breaking through to us, and made otiose, no saving Act from Him actualizing itself in our condition of need. It is this radical dualism that has come to infect the so-called 'new theology' very deeply—that is, something like the old pagan dichotomy between the intelligible and sensible realms, or the old deistic disjunction between an idle God and a mechanistic universe. No doubt the idiom has changed and the context is different, but the basic issues are essentially the same. Now all this means that when you make any statements about God, they do not derive from any real Word that has come to us from the side of God but are interpretations of our own existence in the over-againstness of God to it, so that 'God' becomes only a cipher for our relations with Him. Thus when we speak about God our statements do not really refer to Him for they come up against the hiatus between us and God, and so bend back again to have their meaning within this world alone, in ourselves. Their actual content is our own 'self-understanding'. You do not understand God out of Himself, but out of your own self. That was the fatal step taken by Bultmann in his famous essay of 1925 about the sense in which we can speak of God. But once you have taken that step you cannot stop there; the next is forced on you, when 'God' becomes not so much a cipher of your relations with God but a cipher of your relations with your fellow human beings. And so there emerges the completely secularized man, the man of 'religionless Christianity', who does not resort to prayer because he does not want a 'daddy God' that comes to his help when he is in trouble, for after all he is now a 'mature' human being flung upon his own resources; nor does he need 'the hypothesis of God' or a 'God of the gaps' to help him over the mysterious places in life, for all that is only an 'occult' way of thinking that is primitive.

We need not stop to show the vast confusion there is involved in this way of thinking of the relation between theology and natural science, which is just as pathetic in regard to science as it is in regard to theology. It will be sufficient for our purpose at the moment to make clear the implications of this reductionist view of historic Christianity.

(a) It converts theological statements into anthropological statements and indeed into autobiographical statements. If language about God does not really repose upon an objective revelation of God and is not grounded in an objective reality beyond us, it must be deflected to have only an oblique meaning in ourselves and is to be interpreted only as a symbolic form of human self-expression. Actually this not only cuts man off from God but cuts him off from his neighbour by engrossing him in the depths of his own being. It becomes essentially egotistical. How vastly different is the question of John Robinson, 'How can *I get* a gracious neighbour?', from the question of Jesus, '*Who was neighbour* to him that fell among thieves?'!

(b) It entirely alters the meaning of 'act of God'. This becomes very clear in Bultmann's view of the 'paradoxical' relation between God and the world in which the act of God is found 'at the end of the world', that is, where this world ceases to be, or at the frontier between being and non-being. This is what he means by 'eschatological'. And so Bultmann rejects the fact that the act of God is an objective event *within* our world and is bold and consistent enough therefore to say that the love of God is not a fact within our cosmic existence. Hence the 'act of God' in the death of Christ is no different from the 'act of God' in a fatal accident on the street. Thus with one stroke he eliminates atonement as 'hodge-podge'.

(c) It divides 'Jesus' from 'the Christ' and lets each man substitute himself in the place of Jesus. The radical dualism that lies behind this way of thinking in its Cartesian form led eventually to the fateful disjunction between two kinds of history, which Bultmann and his friends call 'Historie' and 'Geschichte', that is, a scientific reconstruction of historical events operating with the principle of a closed continuum of cause and effect, which eliminates the actual historical Jesus almost completely and certainly makes Him of no account for faith; and an interpretative account of history in which Christ stands for the way the Early Church creatively expressed its orientation to 'other-wordly' reality, and so becomes the point at which we in our generation may through 'faith' gain an authentic relation to existence. The idiom in the thought of Paul Tillich is different, but he makes it equally clear that we have to 'sacrifice Jesus' in order to get 'the Christ'; but when 'the Christ' is detached altogether from the historical Jesus, He becomes a symbol which *we* have to fill with content from ourselves. And so historic Christianity is reduced to a pietistic individualism in which each man fills the symbol of 'Christ' with his own 'self-understanding'.

We have now come to the point where we must not only take stock of these problems that have emerged in modern theology but indicate the way ahead. It must be made clear, however, that while the aberrations we have been discussing have certainly caught the public eye and are being given wide-spread discussion, they by no means represent what is going on in the central march of Christian theology through the centuries. Just as so often it is the sensational material about marriage and divorce that finds its way into the headlines in the popular press, but little is said about the vast host of happy and successful marriages in the lives of our people; so here concentration upon the more outrageous stuff that appears on the outer edges of Christian thought can give a false impression of what has been happening in the steady progress of scientific theology.

It is worthwhile reminding ourselves again of the profound interaction between theological and scientific method that is to be found at the beginning of our modern era in the sixteenth and seventeenth centuries, for whether we like it or not the whole of the future will be dominated by empirical science and anything that fails to stand up to its rigorous discipline will fall away. It is just at this point that the gravamen of our charge against the so-called 'new theology' lies, that at all the four points of scientific reorientation and advance we have noted, it has failed in method and retreated from the truth. It is characterized by a romantic naturalism that is the antithesis of a philosophy of order and design; it represents a flight from hard, exact thinking into the irrational confusion of the 'double-think'; and it registers a reactionary revolt against science into the incoherent flux of existentialism. But in and behind it all, one can hear the old demonic whisper, 'Ye shall be as gods', that it, the original sin of the human subject in projecting himself into the place of ultimate reality, thus rejecting God by eclipsing Him from himself. But in so doing man deprives himself of the light in which to see his own mistakes, and so becomes incarcerated in the darkness of his own self-deception.

What, then, of the way ahead? Whatever else we do we must think out more carefully and stringently the interrelation of object and subject and build into our thinking remedies for the inveterate preoccupation with ourselves from which we all suffer. Here it may serve our purpose to concentrate upon one or two basic simplicities.

You know something only in accordance with its nature, and you develop your knowledge of it as you allow its nature to prescribe for you the mode of rationality appropriate to it. That is the kind of objectivity we adopt in all rational behaviour whatsoever. Thus I adopt toward another person quite a different mode of rationality from that which I adopt toward my desk, because his nature is different from that of a desk. Hence it would be quite irrational or unscientific to treat him like a block of wood or to treat the desk as if it were a human being. That is simple enough, yet its implications are profound and far-reaching. Thus it would be utter nonsense for me to try to know God in the mode in which I know a creature or to treat Him as if He were a star. To know God, I must enter into the mode of rationality prescribed by the nature of God. But it also follows that if we are to know some object in accordance with its nature, it is that same nature that must prescribe the mode of its verification. You cannot demonstrate something in the realm of the mind by chemical analysis, or appreciate the weight of an argument by a machine that weighs things, any more than you can smell with your ear or determine the sound of something by your eyes. Thus the only kind of evidence for God that will satisfy us is one appropriate to divine nature, appropriate to one who is the ground of His own Being and the Source of all other being, to one whose Being is Spirit and whose nature is love.

It is this profoundly simple fact, that knowledge of something and the demonstration of its reality must be in accordance with its nature, that lies behind the formation and deployment of the supreme instrument in all scientific knowledge, *the appropriate question*. If you ask only biological questions you will get only biological answers. If you ask only psychological or anthropological questions, you will only get answers that correspond to them. If you are to get theological answers you must ask theological questions. What is demanded of us in every science, and not least in theology, is strict and accurate thinking in which we learn to ask our questions with unswerving appropriateness and exactitude. It is not easy to ask true questions of God because no question that we can frame is adequate to Him, yet it is not a wrong question because it falls short of Him. But there can be little doubt that many of the difficulties that have been injected into modern theology are due to a real failure to ask the right questions. False questions only falsify the issues, and so no answers to false questions can be given except false ones. That was the point of Immanuel Kant's warning long ago, that we cannot extrapolate modes of thought developed in one science into the operations of another without distortion and falsification. It is often at this point that the 'new theologians' are so strikingly amateurish in the way they mix things up and create pseudo-problems. We must ask them to think scientifically, and to learn to be mature and self-critical in the way they ask their questions.

The progress of our science is the progress we achieve in asking questions. Genuinely scientific questions are questions that lead to new knowledge, questions that are open to the disclosure of what has not been known before. That kind of question needs to be quite open; but to be open it must let itself be called in question in case it is closed from behind by the presuppositions from which it started. Thus the art of asking scientific questions is to ask them in such a way that the question lets itself be questioned in order that it may be re-framed in a way more appropriate to the nature of what is being investigated. Our greatest difficulty, however, lies in the fact that we cannot divorce our questions from ourselves who ask them, for we are part of the questions we ask. Hence to ask scientific questions we ourselves must come into question along with our questions—that means, we with all our preconceptions and our prior self-understanding. To learn what is new we have to learn how to forget; to take a step forward in discovery we have to renounce ourselves. The more rigorously and ruthlessly we pursue our inquiry scientifically the more we ourselves are brought under control. Thus the eclipse of the object by the interposition of ourselves, the obscuring of God through our own subjectivity, is called into question. We become emancipated from imprisonment in ourselves and learn to distinguish the reality of God from our own subjective states and conditions.

It is part of the Christian message that this is possible only through following Jesus Christ, for He alone can put to us the true questions that make us free for the truth. Through His forgiveness He sets us free from ourselves; through taking our place where we are questioned by God, He enables us to renounce ourselves and take up the Cross in following Him; by making us share in His life and what He has done with our human nature in Himself, He turns us away from the false habits of mind in which we are stuck, and transforms us through a renewal of mind that enables us to look away from ourselves to love God with all our heart and mind, and our neighbour as ourselves. But it is only through this encounter with Jesus Christ in His implacable objectivity in which we become crucified to the world and to ourselves that we are enabled to know objectively as we are known by Him and so to think appropriately of God in accordance with His nature, and not out of a centre in ourselves in which we impose our own patterns of thought upon Him and then fail to distinguish Him in His reality from our own subjective states and conditions.

It is only in and through Jesus Christ that man's eclipse of God can come to an end and he can emerge again out of darkness into light.

Looked at in this way, it appears again that the supreme difficulty with the 'new theology' is its axiomatic assumption of a radical dualism between God and the world in which (a) it rejects from the outset any notion of God Himself in His own Being as present and active in our human existence in space and time, so that incarnation, atonement, and resurrection have to be entirely reinterpreted in some oblique symbolic way; and (b) it throws the religious subject back upon himself, so that all his thinking is poised upon his own *sacro egoismo*, while the content of divine revelation is reduced to the conceptions and artefacts that are creatively produced out of his own self-understanding. This is a condition from which he is unable to extricate himself, since it is precisely from himself that he requires to be delivered. It is only Jesus Christ who can do that, for He is the one point in our human and historical existence where we may be lifted out of ourselves and escape the self-incarcerating processes of human subjectivism. But if someone here claims in any way to be a theologian, we may surely ask of him, in a scientific age, to leave adolescent preoccupation with self-exploration and self-fulfilment behind, and to become man enough to engage in the unrelenting processes of scientific questioning in which he himself will be questioned down to the very roots of his existence and so is made open at least to listen for something beyond the echo of his own thought, if not actually to hear a Word coming to him from beyond which he could never tell to himself.

3

Cheap and Costly Grace[1]

Grace is not cheap but costly, costly for God and costly for man, but costly because it is unconditionally free: such is the grace by which we are justified in Christ Jesus. That is the theme which Karl Barth set himself to work out insistently and unambiguously in the famous second edition of his commentary on the Epistle to the Romans, which had such a shattering effect on religion and theology between the two world wars, but which many people have recently picked out of the pages of Dietrich Bonhoeffer without adequately understanding it. Because God has concluded us all under His mercy and justified us freely through grace, all men are put on the same level, for whether they are good or bad, religious or secular, within the Church or of the world, they all alike come under the total judgement of grace, the judgement that everything they are and have is wholly called into question simply by the fact that they are saved by grace alone. This grace is infinitely costly to God because it is grace through the blood of Christ, but it is desperately costly to man because it lays the axe to the root of all his cherished possessions and achievements, not least in the realm of his religion, for it is in religion that man's self-justification may reach its supreme and most subtle form.

How did the Reformers understand justification by grace? Normally they expounded it as justification by faith, partly because of the Pauline usage which was given such decisive exposition by Luther in his discussion of the epistles to the Romans and

[1] Reprinted from *The Baptist Quarterly*, Vol. XXII, No. 6, April 1968, pp. 290–311.

Galatians, but also to stress the contrast between 'faith' and 'works'. Understood in this way 'faith alone' was the correlative of 'grace alone' but before long it became apparent that the notion of 'justifying faith' was highly ambiguous. This made it easy for the opponents of Reform to caricature the Lutheran doctrine of justification, but was the Council of Trent entirely wrong when it accused it of turning faith into a justifying work? History has proved the fathers of Trent shrewder than was realized at the time, for this is exactly what happened again and again in the development of Lutheran and Reformed Theology alike, when it was taught that men and women are justified by God's grace *if* they repent and believe. Thus there arose the concept and practice of *conditional grace* which permeated Protestantism, Lutheran Pietism, and the Federal Theology of the Calvinists, Puritanism and Anglicanism alike. The Romans had taught that we need first of all an infusion of supernatural grace for without it we can do nothing, but that must be given to us *ex opere operato*, that is, without any co-operation on our part. Once it is received, however, we may co-operate with divine grace in living the Christian life, meriting more grace through repentance and obedience and receiving it through the sacraments. The Reformers rightly attacked this quantitative notion of grace and exposed the Pelagian heresy latent in the Roman notion of merit, for it obscured the Gospel of free forgiveness of sins granted on the merits of Christ alone. But as soon as righteousness and life were thought of as offered to us by God under the condition of faith the old errors crept back to corrupt the evangelical message and a new legalism resulted. Nowhere perhaps has this difficult ambiguity in historical Protestantism come out more sharply than in the controversies that arose with the publication of *The Marrow of Modern Divinity in* 1645 and 1649. In Scottish theology it received its most trenchant exposure from the pen of James Fraser of Brea in *A Treatise on Justifying and Saving Faith* (not published until 1722) in which he rejected the whole notion of conditional redemption and attacked the legalizing of the Gospel that came from making 'justifying faith' into a saving work. He sought instead to ground faith upon the active obedience of Christ and His complete sufficiency for

our justification, which gave rise to an unconditionally free proclamation of the Gospel.

This difficulty is just as evident in our own times, for Evangelical
Protestantism has developed a way of preaching the Gospel which
distorts and betrays it by introducing into it a subtle element of
co-redemption. This happens whenever it is said that people will
not be saved *unless* they make the work of Christ real for themselves by their own personal decision, or that they will be saved
only if they repent and believe, for this is to make the effectiveness
of the work of Christ conditional upon what the sinner does, and
so at the crucial point it throws the ultimate responsibility for a
man's salvation back upon himself. That is very far from being
Good News for the sinner, for he knows well that if everything
depends at last on the weak link that he must add to the chain of
salvation then he is utterly lost. The message of the New Testament is quite different. It announces that God loves us, that He
has given His only Son to be our Saviour, that Christ has died
for us when we were yet sinners, and that His work is finished,
and *therefore* it calls for repentance and the obedience of faith, but
never does it say: This is what God in Christ has done for you,
and you can be saved on condition that you repent and believe.
The Gospel must be preached in an evangelical way, that is, in
accordance with the nature and content of the Gospel of free
grace, else it is 'another Gospel'. It is not faith that justifies us,
but Christ in whom we have faith. But the history of Protestantism shows that it is possible to speak of justification by faith in
such a way that the emphasis is shifted from 'Christ' to 'me', so
that what becomes finally important is 'my faith', 'my decision',
'my conversion', and not really Christ Himself. This is partly
what has led to the modern notion of salvation by *existential
decision*, in which we interpose ourselves, with our faith and our
decision, in the place of Christ and His objective decision on our
behalf.

Think, for example, of the change that has come over the conception *Christus pro me* between Luther and Bultmann. For Luther
the *pro me* referred to the objective intervention of God in Christ,
a saving act independent of man himself by which he is liberated

even from himself, for there is nothing that man can do by way of knowledge or decision or believing that can deliver him from his in-turned, self-centred self. He distinguished the *pro me*, therefore, sharply from a mere belief that something is true. Just as in the Holy Communion he refused to translate the *est* in *Hoc est corpus meum* by *significat* so he refused to translate the *pro me* merely by 'what it means for me'. While faith has its proper place in justification it is faith that rests entirely on the objective fact proclaimed by the Gospel that Jesus Christ was put to death for our trespasses and raised for our justification. But with Bultmann the *pro me* is very different, for all statements that in the New Testament speak of what *God has done for me* are transposed to speak only of what *He means for me*. Now of course the *pro me* of Luther also includes the *significance* of what God has done *for me*, because in Christ God has taken an objective decision on my behalf that means something for me, but for Bultmann it is just this objective act that must be dropped altogether in order to get the meaning of it 'for me'. Thus the death of Jesus on the Cross is merely something that happened in the closed connection of cause and effect and that has no meaning for us, but there is another event that may have meaning, the *kerygma* or preaching of the apostles about this event, which we must apply to ourselves. Thus for Bultmann interpretation of the New Testament is the same as giving it a meaning for myself now in my own contemporary situation; but I cannot do that, he argues, if I concentrate upon something that actually took place in the past, for that can only introduce doubts and destroy faith. Rather must I be prepared to give up any attempt at the kind of security that finds for faith an objective act of God in history, and take the road of radical decision in which I work out the meaning for myself in the present.

This is what he means by justification by faith, but it would be hard to think of anything so opposed to Luther's teaching at the Reformation when he spoke of justification as taking place *extra nos* and of the righteousness bestowed upon us in the free gift of God as *aliena justitia*, all in order to show that it does not arise out of what we do and is not invested with any significance that we think up for ourselves. Justification is through *Jesus Christ alone*, while faith is the divine gift of trust and reliance on what Christ has done in which we are caught up out of ourselves and planted in Him. But for Bultmann this relation between faith and what Christ has actually done is snapped, for 'faith' has become man's own human act, his existential decision, the process by which he gives meaning to the *kerygma* for himself in the present. This concentration upon the meaning of the Gospel as what it means for me, in detachment from objective acts of God in our world and in detachment from historical events in the past, imports an astounding egocentricity in which the significance of the *pro me* is shifted entirely from its objective to its subjective pole. And so we see justification by grace being turned into its exact opposite.

This is why Karl Barth put as his fundamental question to Bultmann, that which asks whether the *kerygma* as Bultmann expounds it is really a Gospel at all, Glad Tidings of utterly free grace and divine justification beyond anything that we can do of ourselves. The great lesson to be learned from this is that whenever we take our eyes off the centrality and uniqueness of Jesus Christ and His objective vicarious work, the Gospel disappears behind man's existentialized self-understanding, and even the Reality of God Himself is simply reduced to 'what He means for me' in the contingency and necessities of my own life purpose.

Let us consider then what is involved in justification by Christ alone. It means that it is Christ, and not we ourselves, who puts us in the right and truth of God, so that He becomes the centre of reference in all our thought and action, the determinative point in our relations with God and man to which everything else is made to refer for verification or justification. But what a disturbance in the field of our personal relations that is bound to create! Many years ago when I read a well-known book on *The Elements of Moral Theology* I was astonished to find that Jesus Christ hardly came into it at all. He had been thrust into a corner where He could hardly be noticed, while the ethical and indeed the casuistical concern dominated the whole picture. But what emerged was an ethic that was fundamentally continuous with our ordinary natural existence and was essentially formal. How different altogether,

I thought, was the ethical disturbance that attended the teaching and actions of Jesus or the upheaval that broke in upon contemporary society and law when He proclaimed the absolutes of the Kingdom of God, and summoned people to radical obedience.

What happened when Jesus came upon the scene has been very memorably expounded by Bultmann in his little book that bears the English title *Jesus and the Word*. What He challenged was the formalization of the Will of God in the Jewish Ethic which came to be concerned with the authoritative commandments as such rather than with their content, but it was the content that determined whether a commandment was really God's will or not. Bultmann then shows from the teaching of Jesus that when obedience is simply subjection to a formal commandment or authority, the human self need not be essentially committed. What man does is to yield accidental conformity while he himself remains neutral, finally untouched by the divine claim. In this kind of decision he stands outside of his action; he is not completely obedient. It is precisely this detachment and neutrality that Jesus broke through in His call for radical obedience, in which man's inner being is brought to assent to what is required of him; he decides to act in such a way that he is completely committed to his decision for his whole self stands behind what he does. It is only with such a radical obedience, Bultmann claims, that a genuine ethic is to be conceived, for then man is forced out from his hiding-place behind formal law and authority and is made fully responsible for his actions. There cannot be any doubt that this is what Jesus did, and St. Paul followed Him closely in this; but it is just at this point that Bultmann's understanding falls radically short of the Gospel of justification by Christ, for he insists that man is then thrown entirely upon himself in regard to the judgements of good and evil, so that he himself is made responsible in every new decision for what is to be done. That is to say, after his magnificent analysis of what Jesus taught face to face with the authority of the Scribes and Pharisees, he throws man back finally upon himself as the sole bearer of responsibility, whereas what the Gospel of Jesus proclaims is that God Himself has stepped into our situation and made Himself responsible for us in a way that sets our life on a wholly new basis.

We may express that in another way. What Jesus did, according to Bultmann, was to think out radically to the end the absolute requirement of man within the relation between what he 'is' and what he 'ought to be' and so made everything pivot upon man's own individual decision. But there is no suggestion of a Gospel that Jesus Christ has to come to lift man out of that predicament in which even when he has done all that it is his duty to do he is still an unprofitable servant, for he can never overtake the ethical 'ought'. But actually the Gospel is the antithesis of this, for it announces that in Jesus Christ God has already taken a decision about our existence and destiny in which He has set us upon the ground of His pure grace where we are really free for spontaneous ethical decisions toward God and toward men. This means that the decision to which man is summoned in the *kerygma* of Jesus is one that reposes upon the prior and objective decision that He has taken on our behalf and which He announces to us freely and unconditionally. What is completely disastrous in Bultmann's ethic is that it rejects the objective decision, the actualized election of grace, upon which the whole of the Christian Gospel rests, so that in the last analysis he can only promulgate an ethic which, 'radical' though it may be, is only a prolongation of man's already existing experience and a reduction of it to what his previous knowledge includes, or at any rate could acquire through philosophical analysis. This is only to incarcerate man in the end quite cruelly in his own existentialized self-understanding, for there is no divinely provided fulcrum whereby he may be lifted out of the prison-house of himself and his own naturalistic existence, no really objective Christ, no vicarious Saviour.

Justification by Christ, however, is something very different. It means that God Himself has intervened in our ethical predicament where our free-will is our self-will and where we are unable to extricate ourselves from the vicious moral circle created by our self-will, in order to be selflessly free for God or for our neighbour in love. It means that God has interacted with our world in a series of decisive events within our historical and moral existence in which He has emancipated us from the thraldom of our own failure and redeemed us from the curse of the law that held us in such bitter bondage to ourselves that we are now free to engage in obedience to His will without secondary motives, but also so free from concern for ourselves and our own self-understanding that we may love both God and our neighbour objectively for their own sakes. It is thus that justification involves us in a profound moral revolution and sets all our ethical relations on a new basis, but it happens only when Christ occupies the objective centre of human existence and all things are mediated through His grace.

Before we proceed further let us pause to ask how it has come about that in the Churches that stemmed from the Reformation, the mighty Saviour, Jesus Christ, could be reduced to the vanishing point that He is given in the existentialist re-interpretation of the Gospel. It looks as though it developed out of our persistent Protestant attempt to interpret Christ solely through His works. 'This is to know Christ, to know His benefits', as Melanchthon expressed it. When you start off from the saving work of Christ like that and from what He means to you in your experience, Christ Himself tends to disappear behind His benefits, so that a doctrine of the person of Christ is determined by the value-judgements you pass on Him. Or to express it more doctrinally, when the atonement is limited in our thought only to what Christ did in His death on the Cross while the incarnation and the incarnate life of the Son of God are treated only as a prelude or as a necessary means for atonement, then a proper Christology concerned with the nature and person of the Son of God tends to fall away. But when atonement itself is not rooted ontologically in Christ or in God Himself, then it becomes what the Germans call *Ereignistheologie*, a theology of events. Thus the saving benefits of Christ in which we rejoice, becoming detached from His personal Being, rapidly degenerate into timeless events with no essential relation to history. That is what we see happening very clearly in the Ritschlian background to Bultmann's thought; but when the *kerygma* of saving events is detached from historical facticity like that, we are inevitably thrown back upon ourselves, so that we interpret it out of our own existence in the concrete circumstances in which we are involved. Then we read out of it only what we have first read into it.

It becomes clear, therefore, that what we require to recover is an understanding of justification which really lets Christ occupy the centre, so that everything is interpreted by reference to who He was and is. After all, it was not the *death* of Jesus that constituted atonement, but Jesus Christ the Son of God offering Himself in sacrifice for us. Everything depends on *who* He was, for the significance of His acts in life and death depends on the nature of His Person. It was *He* who died for us, *He* who made atonement through His one *self*-offering in life and death. Hence we must allow the Person of Christ to determine for us the nature of His saving work, rather than the other way round. The detachment of atonement from incarnation is undoubtedly revealed by history to be one of the most harmful mistakes of Evangelical Churches. Nowhere is this better seen, perhaps, than in a theologian as good and great as James Denney who, in spite of the help offered by James Orr and H. R. Mackintosh, was unable to see the essential interconnection between atonement and incarnation, and so was, on his own frank admission, unable to make anything very much of St. Paul's doctrine of union with Christ. At this point, as Mackintosh pointed out, Denney and Ritschl were at one.

This has certainly been one of the most persistent difficulties in Scottish theology. In Calvin's Catechism we read: 'Since the whole affiance of our salvation rests in the obedience which He has rendered to God, His Father, in order that it might be imputed to us as if it were ours, we must possess Him: for His blessings are not ours, unless He gives Himself to us *first*.' It is only through union with Christ that we partake of His benefits, justification, sanctification, etc. That is why in the *Institute* Calvin first offered an account of our regeneration in Christ before speaking of justification, in order to show that renewal through union with Christ belongs to the inner content of justification; justification is not merely a judicial or forensic event but the impartation to us of Christ's own divine–human righteousness which we receive through union with Him. Apart from Christ's incarnational union with us and our union with Christ on that ontological basis, justification degenerates into only an empty moral relation. That was also the distinctive teaching of the Scots Confession. But it was otherwise with the Westminster Confession, which reversed the order of things: we are first justified through a judicial act, then through an infusion of grace we live the sanctified life, and grow into union with Christ. The effects of this have been extremely damaging in the history of thought. Not only did it lead to the legalizing, or (as in James Denney's case) a moralizing of the Gospel, but gave rise to an 'evangelical' approach to the saving work of Christ in which atonement was divorced from incarnation, substitution from representation, and the sacraments were detached from union with Christ; sooner or later within this approach where the ontological ground for the benefits of Christ had disappeared, justification became emptied of its objective content and began to be re-interpreted along subjective lines. It is because this is the state in which so many people in this country find themselves today that they become such easy prey for the reductionist notions of the Gospel that reach us from the Continent. We Protestants require to go back in our tracks in order to recover something we lost in our reaction against Roman error, how to interpret the work of Christ from His Person rather than the other way round. Unless we do that we will inevitably interpret both the work and the person of Christ from out of ourselves.

There is a further aspect of justification by grace that requires to be considered. By putting us completely in the right or the truth with God, Christ calls us completely into question. That is the offence of Jesus that the Evangelists were not slow to point out, for the way in which He embodied the love of God among men or expounded to them what the Kingdom of God was like so often rebuffed them. Parable after parable, saying after saying, shocked them terribly, while the kind of person He was and the kind of ministry He exercised cut deeply into their pride, their knowledge, their religion, and their most cherished desires. By bringing the Kingdom of divine grace to bear directly upon their lives He revealed the vast chasm between the heart of man and the Will of God, for it provoked the bitter hostility of man to God and brought Jesus to the Cross. Yet in His suffering and passion He launched God's supreme attack upon man's self-centredness, self-concern, self-security, self-seeking, and self-will. What Jesus did could not be bent to serve the will of men, for He remained to the very end the absolute grace of God that will only be grace and nothing but grace, immutably, unrelentingly, invincibly sheer grace: 'Father, forgive them, for they know not what they do.' By pouring forth upon men unconditional love, by extending freely to all without exception total forgiveness, by accepting men purely on the ground of the divine grace, Jesus became the centre of a volcanic disturbance in human existence, for He not only claimed the whole of man's existence for God but exposed the hollowness of the foundations upon which man tries to establish himself before God. That is precisely what St. Paul meant by speaking of justification as the shattering revelation that God alone is true and every man a liar.

This is most apparent in the realm of our moral life, where the very fact that all men are justified freely by grace concludes them all alike in the solidarity of sin and judgement. It is the uncondi-tional nature of justification that gives it a ruthless radicality in presenting every man before God as a needy sinner, for it is only the sinner that is justified and forgiven. The absolute measure of the forgiveness is the absolute measure of the judgement of divine mercy. That is why we are saved not by the works that we do but by faith that flees from what we do to find refuge alone in what Christ has done for us. That is why at Holy Communion we feel shame for our whole being, for our good as well as for our evil: before the Body and Blood of Christ we have no good-ness to protest, but can plead only the merits of the Saviour. Before the bar of such grace we are searched and judged through and through, where God is Just and Justifier of the ungodly.

This is equally true in the realm of our knowledge, for all thought and statement are justified or verified by reference to Christ alone, from a sole ground in the pure grace of God and not from a ground in ourselves. This means that the Gospel of grace cannot be made understandable by reducing it to what our previous knowledge already includes, as Bultmann insists, or that the divine revelation is to be justified and even legitimized through assimilation to the basic forms of self-understanding that we acquire apart from it. What it does mean is that God's self-revelation makes contact with us not by appealing to some criterion of truth at our disposal but solely out of its own resources. It is to be apprehended therefore out of itself, in accordance with its nature and in the light of its actual happening in our midst and through a conceptual assent which we are forced to yield to it under its own self-evidence. But this means that we come to knowledge only as we are wholly brought into question, so that we with our preconceptions and prior knowledge are encircled with questions on every side and every question we ask must itself be questioned, that the Truth of God may break through to us unhindered and undistorted by answers that we think we can give. By being put in the truth with God we are told that Jesus Christ is our truth, that we have to look away from ourselves to Him alone, and therefore dare not boast of a truth of our own. Even when we have done all our duty in thinking and speaking as accurately and exactly as we can, that is, orthodoxly, we confess that Christ alone is true and that we are in untruth. Thus to boast of orthodoxy is to reject justification by grace alone, for to boast of orthodoxy is to claim that we are already in the truth and do not need to be put in the truth by divine grace. It is a form of self-justification in which we claim that we are able to verify and justify our own beliefs and statements, whereas he who really knows the grace of God knows that he is unable to compel God to be the truth of what he says about Him.

This is the epistemological relevance of justification by the grace of God which the Reformers applied to their understanding of traditional theology and their interpretation of the Holy Scriptures. Because they found that justification directed them to Christ to find their right and truth in Him alone, and thus called in question their self-justification, they found that they had to reject the idea that the criterion of truth is lodged in the subject of the knower or the interpreter. In all interpretation of the Scriptures, for example, we are thrown back upon the Truth of the Word of God, which we must allow to declare itself to us as it calls in question all our preconceptions or vaunted authorities. This means that even though we cannot but work within a stream of tradition we must operate only through bringing all our traditional ideas and all prejudicial notions to the criticism of what becomes revealed in our continuing inquiry of the Word of God. That is to say, they found that justification forced them to transfer the centre of authority from the subjectivity of man or the Church to the objectivity of the Truth itself.

No one since the Reformation has applied justification by God's grace alone so radically and daringly to human theologizing as Karl Barth. It means, as he has shown us, that we can never look for the truth in ourselves but must look for it beyond ourselves in God. It means that we can never claim the truth of our own statements, but must rather think of our statements as pointing away to Christ who alone is the Truth. Theological statements do not carry their truth in themselves, but are true in so far as they direct us away from themselves to the one Truth of God. That is why justification remains the most powerful statement of objectivity in theology, for it throws us at every point upon the Reality of God and what He has done for us in Christ, and will never let us rest upon our own efforts. It is therefore from this ground that we must direct our challenge to those 'new theologians' who deliberately make self-understanding the criterion of their interpretation of the Gospel, or who insist upon an anthropocentric starting-point for theological inquiry. If modern science has learned anything from Christianity, it has learned just this, that in any sphere of investigation we understand things out of themselves and according to their natures, and not out of our own preconceived ideas, yet it is this basic principle of science and theology that they sin against so badly.

Once again justification by grace applies also in the realm of religion for it tells us that it is only the forgiving and reconciling presence of God in human religion that can give it reality, and that this is to be found only in Jesus Christ the one Mediator between God and Man. It tells us therefore that human religion has no worth or truth in itself. Since in and through Christ a way really has been opened up into the presence of God for worship in spirit and in truth, all previous religion, or religion outside of Christ, is displaced and relativized, and robbed of any claim to truth in its own self-grounded existence. Justification reveals in fact that religion can be the supreme form taken by human sin, and be, as it were, an inverted form of atheism. That applies no less to the Christian religion in so far as it becomes independent and autonomous, or indeed secular, and therefore as an attempt on the part of man to secure and entrench himself before God. History certainly makes it clear that through sin and self-will the Christian religion, as easily as any other, may be turned into a form of man's cultural self-expression or the means whereby he seeks to give sanction to a socio-political way of life, and even be the means whereby he seeks to justify and sanctify himself before God. As such it is called completely into question along with every non-Christian religion through justification by grace alone.

This was the point made by Karl Barth with such force in his attack upon nineteenth-century religion and the whole conception of theology as the science of religion, as well as his attack upon all self-centred, self-conscious pietistic religion. Just because religion is the supreme possibility of all human possibilities it can become 'the working capital of sin', the chief means by which sin so insinuates itself into human existence that self-understanding becomes man's ultimate concern and the human subject sets himself on the throne of the divine Subject. It is this kind of religion and even the kind of 'God' set up and worshipped by this religion that falls under the axe of justification through Jesus Christ. This is the source of Bonhoeffer's thought which has been so travestied and misused in modern pop-theology in the call for a 'religionless Christianity'. Already in *The Epistle to the Romans* Barth had poured scorn on this 'pseudo-radicalism', that in which people seek to escape from sin by removing themselves from religion and taking up with some other superior thing, for all this is still to work within the self-centred and self-righteous movement of the human spirit that expresses itself in religion.

Let it be granted that God is to be found only 'on the other side of the frontier of religion' or 'only when the end of the blind alley of ecclesiastical humanity has been reached', but the exposure and relativization of religiosity and ecclesiasticism arise only out of justification by Christ where the positive connection between the truth of religion and God has been established by grace, where the religious and the ungodly alike are justified before God, and where therefore religion is not only judged but justified before God, and judged only because it is justified before Him. That to which we are summoned here is a religion of grace in which we live out of God and not out of ourselves, in which everything in religion is justified by reference to Jesus Christ because it can have no justification by reference to itself, where even the Christian religion lives through divine absolution and is made to rest entirely upon the righteousness of God, and therefore where a 'Christianity without Christ' can only vegetate as a religious but empty form of atheism. The Christian religion has its justification either in the name of Jesus Christ or not at all. It is certainly abolished when everything is made to pivot upon man's own self-understanding.

However we think of it, then, justification calls for a radical self-renunciation, a displacement of the self by Jesus Christ, and therefore for a relentless objectivity in which you do not love your neighbour because love is a form of your self-fulfilment, in which you do not think out of your own self-centredness but out of a centre in the incarnate Word who summons you to leave all and follow Him, and in which you do not pray or worship God in your own name or in your own significance but only in the name and significance of Jesus Christ, in which therefore you do not baptize yourself but are baptized out of yourself into Christ, and in which you do not feed upon yourself but feed only upon the Body and Blood of the Lord.

Justification is at once the most easy thing and yet the most difficult thing to understand, for it is the most easy and yet the most difficult to accept. It is easy because it is so utterly free, and therefore so cheap in the sense that it is quite without price or condition; but it is so difficult because its absolute freeness devalues the moral and religious currency which we have minted at such cost out of our own self-understanding. It is too costly for us.

Justification by grace alone is equally difficult for the man in the parish and the man in the university. Luther was surely right when he declared that no matter how clearly and simply you preach justification, the common people react to it like a cow staring at a new gate. But in the teaching of university students I find that the reaction may also be one of anger and resentment when they understand more than they can accept. But everywhere it seems to be true that modern man wants 'cheap grace', grace which does not set a question mark at his way of life or ask him to deny himself and take up the Cross in following Christ, grace that does not disturb his setting in contemporary culture by importing into his soul a divine discontent, but one which will let him be quite 'secular', grace that merely prolongs his already existing religious experience and does not 'spoil' him for existence as a man of the world. It is hardly surprising, therefore, that there should be immense pressure upon the Church to trim and popularize itself in order to get alongside 'modern man' and offer a 'grace' that is comprehensible to him. But a 'grace' that is comprehensible in this way is not the grace of God that breaks in upon us from beyond all human possibility, and a 'Church' that has removed from its proclamation the power to shock is very far from being the Church of Jesus Christ. A 'Christianity' that has become so secular that it is capable of direct communication to the man of the world, as Kierkegaard used to remind us, has become a harmless superficial thing, capable neither of inflicting deep wounds nor of healing them, for it has nothing to say to men which they do not already know and cannot say to themselves in more satisfactory ways. The more the Church tries to get 'with it' the more it makes itself an otiose relic of the past.

This is not to argue that the Gospel does not need to be proclaimed and taught in the language of the day in which people can hear and grasp what is being said. It must be preached in Chinese to the Chinese and in American to the Americans, and with all the clarity and simplicity that is possible, otherwise it will never reach its target, that is, not even begin to offend; but it must be recognized that the evangelical message about the saving acts of God in Jesus Christ will inevitably appear self-contradictory and meaningless if it is commended to people within the framework of their existing natural knowledge. As Michael Polanyi has pointed out to us so often, such a result is inevitable whenever a language that is apposite to one subject matter is used with reference to another altogether different matter. It is just here that much that is said today about the 'supernatural' founders so miserably, for, to continue Polanyi's thought, 'to the extent to which any event can be established in terms of natural science, it belongs to the natural order of things. However monstrous and surprising it may be, once it has been fully established as an observable fact, the event ceases to be regarded as supernatural. . . . It is illogical to attempt the proof of the supernatural by natural tests, for these can only establish the natural aspects of an event and never represent it as supernatural'.[1] What follows from this is not that we must discard the notion of the supernatural as something meaningless in the modern world, for that would imply that we are to preach only what the natural man can take in naturally, but rather to call for the kind of intellectual effort that is required for every attempt to advance from what we already know to what is really new and which cannot be inferred from what we already know or merely fitted into it when we do apprehend it. As in every great scientific advance we have to engage in a desperate struggle with ourselves in order to make the radical shift in meaning that it involves, so we must ask of the modern world to consider what is announced in the Gospel. By its very nature it cannot be apprehended without a profound change in our natural habits of mind, without a desperate struggle with ourselves and our aversion for change, without taking a step forward beyond what can be validated in our ordinary observable experience toward what can be known only out of itself and in accordance with its divine nature. *Deus comprehensus non est Deus*, as Augustine said. Grace that is comprehensible is not grace, for it is the grace of God that can be known only as God Himself is known, out of God and not out of ourselves. That is what justification *by grace* means.

What, then, are we to make of the modern interpretation of

[1] *Personal Knowledge* (Routledge and Kegan Paul, London, 1958), p. 284.

justification, recently advanced again, as God's acceptance of us as adults or mature people? On the face of it, this seems to be in flat contradiction to the teaching of Jesus that unless we become as little children we shall not enter into the Kingdom of Heaven. There is undoubtedly an immense contrast here between the teaching of our Lord and the 'new theology', for He never talked about maturity and adulthood. He spoke rather of childhood and childlikeness, about being born again, about the blessedness of those who received little children in His name, even of the necessity of becoming like 'sucklings' if we are to participate in God's Kingdom. It is not God's acceptance of us as adults, but God's acceptance of us in simplicity where, like children, we are devoid of sophistication and pretentious self-understanding, where we let Christ be everything, and that includes being the mighty Saviour who came to make Himself responsible for us, to shoulder our burdens, and bear away our sins.

But there is more than this in the notion of maturity and adulthood that is now being advanced. Consider what it meant to Dietrich Bonhoeffer. He was a German of the Germans, deeply, desperately concerned for the problem of Germany, for the very soul of his people as it became revealed under the tyranny of Hitler. It is a strange fact that until modern times Germany seems to have lacked a significant martyr: that is, someone who was so committed to his Christian conviction that he was prepared to make himself fully responsible for it to the extent of laying down his life for it. Germans have tended too easily to yield to authority and Lutherans have tended too easily to yield to the State and in the last analysis to bow before its dictates. Like children kept too long under parental control, German Christians had difficulty in making up their own minds. But with the death of Bonhoeffer (who is here a representative figure, for the German Church now has countless martyrs) German believers began to grow up. Bonhoeffer, you remember, and others found themselves forced to take a terrible decision to assassinate Hitler—it must have been far more terrible for Bonhoeffer as a minister of the Gospel than for the others. Bonhoeffer's courage in this affair to be independent, without even 'using God' as an 'external prop' for his faith, his readiness to take a decision and to bear full responsibility for it in death, constituted, so to speak, a moment of destiny, for in him German Christianity came to maturity, and adult man emerged upon the scene, free from the shackles of authority and standing on his own feet. Germany desperately needed that kind of conviction and courage, and it needed someone like Bonhoeffer to embody it and manifest it. Hence, after the catastrophic defeat of two world wars, and the traumatic sense of guilt, disillusionment, and humiliation that followed, the figure of the martyred Bonhoeffer stood out as an archetype for the new man. Yet the tragedy of the situation is that in the malaise of recent years instead of really listening to Bonhoeffer, many German thinkers and writers and Churchmen have come to 'use' Bonhoeffer for their own ends, as a means of objectifying their own self-understanding and as a symbol on which to project their own image of themselves. And they have been aided and abetted in this by people in Britain and the U.S.A. In this way Bonhoeffer's thought has been severely twisted and misunderstanding of him has become rife, especially when certain catch-phrases like 'religionless Christianity' and 'worldly holiness' are worked up into systems of thought so sharply opposed to Bonhoeffer's basic Christian theology, not least his Christology.

But let us try to single out the real point he was making. There are people who worship God to the end of their life not only in a childlike way but in a childish way, purely on the ground of external authority, be it from the Scriptures or the Church. Take away the minister from the congregation and how often the members appear to collapse in their faith. They have been relying on external props and have not really grown up in their faith. It is even possible to 'use God' as a prop like that, to make Him the prop of your own religion, in such a way that you are protected from the searching judgements of God or from being concluded with all the godly and ungodly in the one solidarity of sin under the divine grace. But when justification by grace is taken seriously the ground is completely taken away from your feet, and away with it there goes your own 'religion' and the 'prop-God' that belongs to it. This was Bonhoeffer's way of radicalizing justification by grace alone over against man's own religious self-justification and self-security.

Bonhoeffer was aware of the fact that we have to think on different levels and of the need on each level to think purely and consistently within it, without mixing up our thought on one level with that on another. Thus on the level of natural science we have to think of nature out of nature, exploring and explaining natural processes solely in terms of themselves, without having recourse to some truth from a different level of thought brought in like a *deus ex machina* to help us out at some difficult impasse. Hence we cannot bring God as a working hypothesis into our natural science in order to explain anything in it, both because natural science in its self-limited concern only for what is observable and contingent operates with a methodological exclusion of God, and because God is not a natural fact of the world which is amenable to the kind of experimental testing and control that we employ in natural science. Bonhoeffer held, then, that in all natural knowledge we have to act according to the principle, *etsi deus non daretur*, without reckoning God among the data. Now Bonhoeffer's position rests rightly upon the fact that God Himself means us to look at the world in this way, for this is the kind of world He has created—it has been made in such a way that it is to be known through scientific inquiry out of itself. Thus the detachment of our understanding of the created universe and all that goes on in it from theological opinions is part and parcel of the Christian doctrine of God the Creator. This happens in no other religion, but it does happen in the Christian religion. Hence, to bring in 'God' in order to stem the 'secularization' of human knowledge is not only pointless but is to use 'God' against His will and can only lead into deep confusion. It can only distort our doctrine of God by confounding Him with worldly powers, and alienate men further and further from the living God of the Bible who is to be known only through the Cross and weakness of Jesus Christ but who in Him conquers the power and space of this world. Thus the 'God' that the Christian must learn to do without is the 'God' as *used* by man to justify his own views, the 'God' who is a prop to his self-justification, but not the God of justification

by grace alone. What Bonhoeffer is protesting against here is the
habit of thinking of God and of nature on one and the same level
(or, on two quite separated levels which are merely the obverse
of each other, which amounts to the same thing!)—this is the
error not only of naturalism but also of a false apologetic that
attempts to defend the Christian doctrine of the transcendence of
God on the same plane of thought as that in which we engage
in merely natural knowledge.

But now the question must be raised whether this principle,
etsi deus non daretur, can apply consistently to the level of ethical
thought and behaviour. Are we to engage in moral decisions
without bringing God into them at all, and are we to learn how
to behave in this secularized world in a purely secular way, *etsi
deus non daretur*? That is to say, are we to learn how to live without
God, without prayer, without the supernatural, without any belief
in or thought of the interaction of God with our world? If so,
does this not really mean that we are thrown back fully and finally
upon ourselves? Surely this would be a total misunderstanding of
Bonhoeffer's thought, for he insisted that what he was concerned
with was 'a clearing of the decks for the God of the Bible', and
that the point of departure for *Christian ethics* is not the reality of
one's own self or the reality of the world, but the 'reality of God
as He reveals Himself in Jesus Christ'. As he says in his *Ethics*,
we have to discard the questions 'How can I be good?' 'How can
I do good?' and ask the very different question 'What is the will
of God?' Bonhoeffer starts, like Barth, from the fundamental
principle of the justification of the sinner by grace alone which
makes a man really free for God and his brothers, for it sets his
life on a foundation other than himself where he is sustained by
a power other than his own. Justification by grace alone removes
from us all false props, all reliance upon external authorities, and
all refuge in worldly securities, and throws us not upon ourselves
but upon the pure act of God in His unconditional love, so that
the ethical and the religious life are lived exclusively from a
centre in Jesus Christ. If the principle *etsi deus non daretur* is applied
here, it must be in accordance with the radicalization of justification that we have already discussed in ethics and religion, in which

man is so emancipated from himself that he is genuinely free for spontaneous action toward God and toward his fellow men.

Yet there is an ambiguity here that seems to go back to a peculiarity in Lutheran thought, the sharp distinction between Law and Gospel, or between the two Kingdoms, the Kingdom of this world and the Kingdom of God, the realm of sight and the realm of faith. Although it was not intended in this way by Luther, it had the unfortunate effect of segregating religion as the sphere of inward relations with God from ethics as the sphere of external behaviour falling within the institution of the State. Thus Luther's distinction between Law and Gospel has so often been a pretext for a way of life in which a man can be a committed member of the Church of Christ on the one hand and yet very much a man of the world on the other hand—*etsi deus non daretur*. When this is reinforced by the philosophical assumption of a radical dichotomy between the noumenal and the phenomenal, the spiritual and the sensuous, the other world of God and this world of closed natural existence, then the disjunction between the Christian Gospel and its practical application becomes very wide indeed —which is one of the most regrettable results of Bultmann's ideas in German theological institutions.

Yet this is exactly what Bonhoeffer rejected in ethics and in Christology. He would have nothing to do with the dualism in the 'pseudo-Lutheran' scheme in which the autonomy of the orders of this world is set in opposition to the Law of Christ. He attacked the kind of thinking in two spheres in which there is such a disjunction between them that a man is forced to seek Christ without the world or the world without Christ, or to try to stand in both spheres at once in their division from one another and so to become a man of eternal tension and conflict. Instead of thinking of two separated realities, we are rather to think of the one Reality of God 'which has become manifest in Christ in the reality of this world'.[1] Thus for Bonhoeffer everything pivots upon the fact that in and through the incarnation the Being of God Himself is to be found 'in space and time', for it is by participating in this Christ that we stand at once both in the Reality

[1] *Ethics* (S.C.M. Press, London, 1955), p. 63f.

of God and in the reality of this world. But this involves the rejection of the dualism of Neo-Protestant Christology which, as Bonhoeffer rightly held, was but a recrudescence of the old Greek
antithesis of idea and phenomenon, i.e., the very dichotomy that
belongs to the essence of Bultmann's whole position. This is made
abundantly clear in Bonhoeffer's *Christology*.

Bonhoeffer's ethic is grounded upon this positive Christology
that rejects equally both docetism and ebionitism, the different
forms of error that arise on the assumption of a radical dichotomy,
and instead holds inseparably together the full Godhead and the
full manhood of Jesus Christ. For Bonhoeffer this meant a critical
repudiation of the approach to Christology that had dominated
the nineteenth century, from the side of Christ's saving work and
His influence upon us, and an approach that interpreted the work
of Christ from the nature of His Person, for in that way alone
could the saving work of Christ be grounded ontologically in
His divine Being. The consequence of this for ethics was profound,
for it meant that it had to be rooted both in the Person of Christ
and in His active obedience. As such it is concerned with the way
in which the reality of Christ assumed reality in our world of
space and time, and therefore with the way Christians do not live
'in themselves' and 'on their own account' but in Christ and on
His account. Christian ethic is ontologically structured in Jesus
Christ and therefore participates in and through Him in His vic-
tory over the dualism between two separated spheres. It is because
he took so seriously the incarnation of the Son of God in the space
and time of this world that he insisted 'that there is no real possibility of being a Christian outside the reality of this world and
that there is no really worldly existence outside the reality of
Jesus Christ'. There is no place therefore to which the Christian
can withdraw from the world; rather must he learn to live out
the reality of Christ within it, for it is in that world that He the
Son of God made our reality His own, and made His reality ours.
This lets us see how grotesque the current cult of 'Bonhoeffer' is,
when it resurrects him from the dead dressed up in the stolen
garments of an existentialized and secularizing 'Christianity'
grounded upon the dualistic assumptions that he overthrew.

Now let us return to the principle *etsi deus non daretur* as Bonhoeffer used it, and consider its obverse which is equally true, that when we think theologically we cannot bring in from natural science 'evidence' to help us out at some point of theological difficulty, or 'criteria' by means of which to manipulate the data and to cut out what is not acceptable to 'modern man', for that would involve just as great a confusion of thought as it would be to employ God as a 'stop-gap' in natural science. This is evident, for example, in the way in which Bultmann with an arbitrary scientism sweeps aside a great deal of the material presented in the Biblical witness without even making a respectful attempt to consider it on its own ground or in his own light. The fact is, however, that when he rejects as mythological all those aspects of the Christian faith which are traditionally known as supernatural, he obviously regards them as elements in a primitive, pre-scientific cosmology; that is, he thinks of them *naturalistically* as aspects of a 'world-view', and does not think of them *theologically*. He is so naïvely misled by the imagery often employed by Biblical writers that he misconstrues *theological distinction* as *spatial or cosmological distance*, and then offers to explain statements cast in this form as objectifications or projections out of man's self-understanding. But this confusion in the reference of biblical and theological statements is the result of the naturalistic habit of mind that Bultmann has brought to the biblical material in the first place. That is to say, while he professes to acknowledge the scientific approach in natural science in which we know things out of themselves and according to their natures, he throws away this scientific approach when he moves into the realm of theology, where he will not allow us to interpret Biblical statements about God's action in history, about the incarnation, resurrection, ascension or parousia of the Son of God, *theologically*, in accordance with the nature of the Reality with which we are there concerned. But when Bultmann tumbles so completely into the illogicality of doubting the supernatural because it does not stand up to his natural tests, it becomes obvious that his parade of scientific critique is only a way of advocating his own philosophical assumptions and naturalistic beliefs.

Another obvious example of this confusion in thought is the argumentation of John Robinson in *Honest to God*, in which he agrees readily with Bonhoeffer that we cannot use God as a hypothesis in our worldly knowledge, but calls for an end of theism because he can only conceive of it as making use of a 'God of the gaps'—that is why his fundamental approach to theism makes him caricature it so crudely as involving statements about God as '*a* Being' or as '*a* Person', which traditional theism *never* does. To think of God under the indefinite article like this is not to think of Him theologically in accordance with His divine nature, but naturalistically as One among other, and therefore creaturely, beings and persons. When we say theologically that God exists, 'exists' here is defined by the nature of God, for He exists only as God exists, and so we speak of Him as *the* Supreme Being who is not in a genus with other beings. And when we say theologically that God is person, the kind of 'person' that is meant is determined by who God is, and so we speak of Him as *the* Person, and indeed as the one Source of all personal existence. As Richard of St. Victor and Duns Scotus taught us long ago, the notion of 'person' used of God must be *ontologically* derived from God's own nature, and therefore from the Trinity, and *not* *logically* worked up from general ideas we already hold on other grounds, else we can only speak of God as 'individual substance'. That is to say, in a proper theism we must get the analogical reference of our thoughts and statements about God right, tracing them back to their source in Him, but how can Robinson do that when he thinks of God, it would seem, only in pictures, and theologizes by finding some new picture deemed relevant to 'secular' man, which *we* must put in the place of the old image of God? What is this but thinking by mythological projection out of ourselves? It is doubtless consistent with this that he should think of God as the ground of our being, for this is to think out of a centre in the depth of man rather than out of a centre in God himself—but then how will it ever be possible for such a thinker to distinguish God from himself?

But why is a Christian bishop's thought forced into this mould? It is because he too operates with the philosophical assumption of a radical dualism, superficially concealed but actually revealed by his rejection of 'supranaturalism' and his identification of God with 'the ground of our being'. On the one hand, there is the natural world to which we all belong, secularly understood by closing the circle of explanation and centred in human affairs, but on the other hand there is God understood as 'creative ground and meaning', but God is not thought of as interacting with it in any causal way. Let it be granted that the causal relation between God and the world is of a unique kind, appropriate to the nature of God, and that there are mistaken and misleading ways of speaking of God's transcendence and supernatural activity, nevertheless it seems clear that in insisting upon 'the powerlessness of God' (again pathetically misconstruing Bonhoeffer's thought) Robinson has lapsed into an inverted form of deism which cannot be covered up by his rejection of the deistic caricature. It is all the same for this deistic 'God' whether He is absent like a rich aunt in Australia where He is powerless to intervene, or present in the depth of John Robinson's breast as the significance of his being where He is powerless to save, answer prayer, or even to have mercy, for He is so entangled in the ground of his being that He cannot be other than what Robinson always and actually is in the depth of himself. It is no use his appealing at this point to John Macmurray's statement that God is 'the personal ground of all that we experience' for Macmurray holds that we know truly and rationally only when we know objectively, and that means when we can distinguish what is objectively real from our own subjective states and conditions, and he holds also that it is this objectivity subsisting between our personal relations that is 'the core of rationality'. Thus Robinson's position is more impossible than that of straightforward deism, for he is unable to distinguish God 'out there' rationally as objectively and transcendently other than the depths of his own being, and so he is thrown back upon himself to give content to his notion of God, as what is of ultimate concern *for* him in the depth and significance of his own being. But when he does that by looking about for a new way of speaking about God that will satisfy that concern of his and so get the 'God' that he wants, how can he avoid making God a predicate of himself or 'using God' for his own ends and satisfactions, which is precisely the kind of 'God' that Bonhoeffer exposed as idolatrous projection and that must be given up?

It is evident that the so-called 'new theologians' are out for *cheap grace*, i.e. the 'God' *they* want, one to suit themselves and modern 'secular' man, rather than the God of *costly grace* who calls for the renewing of our minds in which we are not schematized to the patterns of this world but are transformed in conformity with His own self-revelation in Jesus Christ. They balk at Jesus Christ at the crucial point in His message, where He asks them to renounce themselves, take up the cross and follow Him unreservedly all along the road to crucifixion and resurrection. Somehow they feel, rather mistakenly, that the Gospel threatens elements of truth that are very important for them and which they must secure for the modern world. Actually they are far from understanding them properly because they are obstructed in working out their implications through their own self-centredness, and cannot see that what the Gospel threatens is the distortion of them involved in the way they seek to uphold and preserve them. They are indeed important truths, although they have taken a long time to germinate since they broke free from their husks at the Reformation, namely, *the liberation of nature* that comes from taking seriously God's creation of the world out of nothing, and *the affirmation of nature* that comes from the doctrine of grace alone in which God turns, in the unconditional freedom of His love, toward the world which He has made and which He continues in His grace to maintain in its distinctness from Himself and thus in dependence upon Himself. Both of these assert that it is the active and creative relation of God to nature that alone preserves its utter contingency and obstructs its divinization. Cut away that relation to the God of creation and grace and what ensues can only be deism or atheism in some form or other. The confusion of thought that has arisen today can be indicated by pointing out that while these elements of truth gave rise to modern empirical science operating with the principle of objectivity, the new theology smothers them with a massive subjectivity in which there is revealed a reactionary flight from scientific objectivity.

We cannot work out the implications of these important elements of truth here, but two points must be pointed out, that are essential to any serious consideration of them. (1) They tell us that we must learn to think, not in separated spheres, but on different levels at the same time. (2) They tell us also that there must be interaction between the levels, if everything is not to dissolve into meaninglessness. The importance of holding both these together can easily be indicated through the analogy of the hierarchy of levels in language, in mathematics or the various exact sciences, where the openness of each level upwards to the next through interaction with it is absolutely necessary for rational thought, for apart from it we can only engage in playing games at the different levels without any applicability to reality. What I find most of the 'new theologians' doing, however, is cutting away the interaction between the two main levels of thought with which they are concerned, relating to nature and to God, in the crazy idea that only in this way can they preserve the distinctness and significance of each level of thought! Some of them, on the other hand, try to flatten the levels out on to one and the same plane of thought, thus producing impossible contradictions and illogicalities, as would happen, of course, in any science if that were done. Without any doubt the corroding or the eliminating of this interaction between the levels of thought can only lead to utter futility and meaninglessness—and that is what so many of the 'new theologians' are doing, driving the flock of Christ into the chasm of unmeaning.

Now in order to draw our discussion to a close let me illustrate this problem by linking it up again with justification, and considering it in its Lutheran form of *simul justus et peccator*. Here we are thinking on two levels, of the divine act of justification in Christ, and of the existence of the human sinner in this world, at the same time. It was a peculiarity of Luther's exposition of this that he thought of the righteous act of God as set forth *sub contraria specie*, under its contrary aspect, real in Christ and for the sinner in Christ, but hidden under the veil of this visible world. Hence he expounded the relation between the *justus* and the *peccator* in terms of imputation in a dialectical manner. But there is another side to his thought, for justification is the content of the Word of grace that God directs to us, a Word that is mighty, living and active. When God declares in His Word that we are righteous, we *are* righteous, for His Word makes it so. It is not an empty Word but one that fulfils what it declares. Thus there is a creative relation between the *justus* and *peccator*, for God continues to maintain a dynamic relation between Himself and the sinner in such a way that His forgiving and creative Word operates in his being and life. Although it is only by faith that we may properly discern that interaction, it will be revealed in its full reality at the coming of Christ and in the resurrection of the body. But since the reality of justification is grounded in the incarnate person and work of the Son of God, it is continually communicated to us afresh in the real presence of Christ in the bread and wine, so that here and now in our worldly historical existence we may actually partake of it as we have communion in the Body and Blood of Christ. Luther's immense insistence upon 'This *is* my body', against every attempt to reinterpret it as 'This *signifies* my body', is due to his penetrating insight that if the creative interaction between God and the world, between the Son of God and history, or between justifying grace and the ungodly, is weakened or whittled away, the Christian Gospel becomes empty of content and reality.

It has been a constant temptation of Lutheranism, however, especially in modern times, to stress too much the dialectical side of Luther's thought about the divine gift of righteousness as concealed under its contrary worldly aspect, and so to let a merely imputational or forensic relation between *justus* and *peccator* replace a real, dynamic relation, with the result that justification comes to be thought of as an *empty legal fiction*. When that happens anywhere the great Reformation message fizzles out into meaninglessness, while every attempt to fill in the vacuum with stuff derived from man's self-understanding only leads in the end to bitter *ressentiment* and mocking iconoclasm. In this event the wages of the new theology is death, including the most cynical death of all, 'the death of "God"'.

But of course there is quite a different side to Lutheranism, for the 'new theology' belongs only to its modernistic flank. The main teaching of the Lutheran Church is to be found in the central emphasis upon union with Christ, upon the positive, creative relation between the forgiving God and the sinner, upon the presence and activity of the divine Reality in the reality of this world, such as we have seen in the thought of Bonhoeffer, or such as we may see today in the theology of Schlink or Vogel, Skydsgaard or Prenter. But when, as in Bonhoeffer, the dialectical aspect of Justification is sharpened to a cutting edge, as when he speaks about 'the Church as the evil world to the highest degree', or 'worldly holiness', this cannot be used as grist for the mills of the theologies of radical dualism, where it can only be purloined for the expression of 'cheap grace', whereas in Bonhoeffer's thought, as in Luther's, it was meant as the expression of 'costly grace'—that is, of the incredible abasement of God in which He condescended to come Himself in His own personal Being into our world of space and time, and to interact in His grace with worldly men in the depths of their sin and shame, conquering the power of our space and time through His 'weakness' in Jesus, and justifying the ungodly through His 'powerlessness' on the Cross. This is the antithesis of the 'new theology'. Its statements may be linguistically identical with those of Bonhoeffer or of Luther, or even with those of the Holy Scripture, but their meaning is quite different, for the rejection of God's interaction with this world and the assumption of a radical dichotomy between the world of the divine Reality and this world of space and time, gives those statements quite another reference as they are deflected back finally upon man himself for their content.

III THEOLOGY AND SCIENCE

4

Theology in the Scientific World[1]

When modern *a posteriori* science emerged out of the sixteenth century and began its classical development in the seventeenth century it became known as *dogmatic science*, both because it replaced deduction from abstract principles with an inductive method of discovery *directed* by the things into which it inquired, and because it claimed in this way to advance *real* knowledge of the universe. This idea of 'dogmatic' thought was taken over from the old Greek contrast between the 'dogmatics' and the 'sceptics'. In the works of Sextus Empiricus, for example, those philosophers or scientists (they were the same in those days) who asked questions of the kind that yielded positive results were called the *dogmatikoi*, whereas those who asked merely academic questions without any intention of getting positive answers were called the *skeptikoi*. It was in this sense that *dogmatic science* was applied to describe the new physics, as a positive form of science in which a specific field of reality was fenced off from all distracting and speculative questions in order to concentrate inquiry upon the subject-matter itself and derive understanding of it out of its own inner connections and not in accordance with fixed preconceptions or external authorities. Critical questioning was not to be evaded, for acquired habits of thought and new ideas thrown up by inquiry had to be tested; but the inquiry had always to return to the given realities so that the scientist could let his mind fall under the direction of their natural patterns and then formulate in positive 'laws' or 'dogmas' what he was forced to apprehend by the realities themselves.

[1] Lecture given to all Faculties in the University of Edinburgh, 27 November 1968.

89

Dogmatic science, in this sense, was applied later in the seventeenth century to theology, bracketed off as a field of inquiry on its own, unobstructed by abstract questions as to essence or sceptical questions as to possibility before proper scrutiny had been given to the actual nature of the given realities or the actual situation in which knowledge of them arose. Critical and epistemological questions were raised, but only on the ground of actual knowledge, in the light of the inner logic of the material content, and with rigid exclusion of *a priori* assumptions or external presuppositions and authorities. Thus understood theological dogmatics is not a closed, logico-deductive system of knowledge, but an open science, disciplined and controlled by a logic beyond our own minds, and therefore never relieved of the need for critical and positive reconstruction in the light of the truth as our minds become progressively open to it through appropriate inquiry.

It cannot be claimed that theological dogmatics since the seventeenth century has always been pursued in this way, for before long it tended to lapse back into the style and mode of medieval scholastic science. Theological subject-matter became systematized in forms of thought not derived from the actual field of theological inquiry but from a new formalistic Aristotelianism and from the rigid structures that were thrown up in the new mechanistic interpretation of physics. This had the effect of reducing 'dogmatics' to a system of philosophy based on principles dictated by the autonomous reason, or to a system of theology grounded on first principles self-evident to the reason and analytically and logically ordered into a coherent body of truth. From its stress upon positive content and constructive procedure 'dogmatics' came to be understood as philosophical or theological dogmatizing without critical reference to the evidence of primordial realities, while in this changed sense of the term Roman theologians also began to speak of the logico-deductive presentation of conciliar decisions and Church dogmas as 'dogmatics'. Thus dogmatics became assimilated to rationalistic assumptions and external authorities from which as a science it had earlier been emancipated. It was, of course, out of this later development that the notion of 'dogmatism' arose, i.e. the narrow, opinionated thinking characteristic of the closed mind and the way of laying down statements that goes with it.

In our day, however, there has taken place a powerful rehabilitation of dogmatics in its strictest sense, as *pure science*. In it we seek to advance our actual knowledge of things through open inquiry in such a way that they become revealed to us in their own inner connections and are apprehended in their own self-explication, i.e. as a science submitting only to the demands of its own subject-matter and operating in terms of the inner law of its own being. Hence a dogmatic science of this kind, whether it be in physics or theology, cannot allow another department of knowledge working in quite a different field to dictate to it on its own ground, either in prescribing its methods or in predetermining its results—that would be the bad sort of dogmatizing which unfortunately theology encounters today not infrequently from 'scientism' and from philosophical 'empiricism'. Rather does each science allow its own subject-matter to determine how knowledge of it is to be developed, since method and subject-matter may not be separated. Thus by engaging in dogmatics theology claims to be objective knowledge exhibiting its own grounds and developing the forms, possibilities, and conditions of knowledge proper to the distinctive realities of its own field. It is knowledge which can and must be pursued rigorously as a science.

There are not two ways of knowing, a scientific way and a theological way. Neither science nor theology is an esoteric way of knowledge. Indeed because there is only one basic way of knowing we cannot contrast science and theology, but only natural science and theological science, or social science and theological science. In each we have to do with a fundamental act of knowing, not essentially different from real knowing in any field of human experience. Science is the rigorous and disciplined extension of that basic way of knowing and as such applies to every area of human life and thought. It should be clear, then, that I am not using 'science' in the vulgar sense to mean only natural science, and certainly not within natural science as limited to physics. I am using 'science' to denote the critical and controlled extension of our basic modes of rational activity with a view to positive knowledge.

In a science we know some given reality strictly in accordance with its nature, and we let its nature determine for us the form and content of our knowledge of it. We cannot assume that we already know what its nature is, for we learn what it is only through inductive questioning in which we try to let it declare itself to us in spite of, and often in contradiction to, what we tell ourselves about it. This is a process in which we find ourselves being stripped of our preconceived ideas. Our main difficulty in learning is undoubtedly with ourselves and our built-in habits of thought which we stubbornly carry over from the past or from another area of knowledge into our inquiries but which can only obstruct and distort our apprehension of what is really new. In scientific activity we let ourselves and what we think we already know be called in question, so that as far as possible we may know the given reality out of itself and in accordance with its own nature. We know natural processes, for example, not out of *a priori* assumptions, but by exploring natural processes alone, and by thinking of them only in terms of natural processes and through forms of thought which we develop under the pressure of what they actually are. In scientific activity of this kind we try to ground our knowledge of the given reality squarely upon the reality itself and articulate what we know out of a compelling and exclusive relation with it. This means that we must distinguish what we know from our subjective states and conditions and that in proportion as we know something in accordance with its own nature we allow our presuppositions to be suspended or set aside. But it also means that we must learn to distinguish what we know from our knowing of it, so that we may not confuse our forms of knowledge with the realities we apprehend through them. What all this adds up to is the principle of scientific objectivity, which is simply an extension of our fundamental rationality in which we think and act in accordance with what is the case. Is it needless to stress once again that this is the antithesis of objectifying modes of thought in which we project upon what we seek to know elaborations out of our own consciousness?

Furthermore: in all scientific knowledge, we let the nature of what we know prescribe for us the specific mode of rationality we adopt toward it. That is why in every science we operate with a distinctive form of inquiry proper to the nature of the object we investigate in it. The kind of inquiry we develop in our investigation of determinate objects, for example, takes the form of physical questioning or experiments in which we force mute nature to answer our questions, or, to use Bacon's expression, in which we have to 'torment' nature in order to elicit a 'yes' or 'no' in reaction to our stipulations. But when we are concerned to know personal objects, or subjects, we adopt quite a different form of inquiry in which physical compulsion is entirely out of place, one in which personal reciprocity in speaking and listening, asking and answering, is the appropriate mode of rationality. We have to reckon, of course, with the fact that our different fields of inquiry overlap each other, but the fact that in each science such precision is required of us that we have to develop a distinctive vocabulary apposite to the nature of the realities in its field, is evidence of the fact that from field to field there takes place a considerable shift in the mode of our rationality. Again, it is because the nature of what we know prescribes for us the specific mode of rationality that we adopt toward it, that it also prescribes for us the proper mode of its verification. I cannot test whether there is a bad smell about by my ear. I cannot verify the presence of a chemical element in some compound by religious experience. Nor can I demonstrate a proposition in astrophysics by some line of reasoning in aesthetics. All that would obviously be irrational, just as irrational as it would be to put God to the test in the same sort of way in which we put nature to the test in carrying through a physical experiment or to demand of Him that He disclose His reality to us through a radar telescope. In view of all this it is not surprising that theology, if only out of scientific necessity, requires of us a mode of rational inquiry appropriate to the nature of its distinctive object, with its own suitable and significant vocabulary, and its own proper mode of verification, in accordance with the nature of its object and its distinctive rationality.

Here is something that needs to be emphasized. In every science we presuppose that what we know is accessible to rational inquiry, that it is somehow inherently intelligible or rational. If it were not, there could be no knowledge, let alone any science. Hence a primary operation that must be undertaken in any science, e.g. in developing verification, is to probe into the inner rationality of the object or field of knowledge, into its inner logic. Of course, if we cannot do that, we are entitled to question whether we are working in a genuine field of knowledge and whether what is claimed to be knowledge is not just something thought up out of our own subjectivities and projected out there in an objectified form. But if we can bring to view the inner rationality of a field of knowledge, we are convinced that we are in touch with reality, that we are not inventing but discovering, that we are thinking as we are compelled to think by the essential nature of the realities themselves.

Let us reflect upon this more fully. What the scientist does in any field is to seek to achieve an orderly understanding of events in which he can grasp them as a connected and intelligible whole and so be able to penetrate into their inner rationality. He does not invent that rationality but discovers it, even though he must act with imagination and insight in detecting and developing the right clues and act creatively in constructing forms of thought and knowledge *through* which he can discern the basic rationality and let his thinking fall under its direction as he offers even a descriptive account of the events. Undoubtedly a two-way movement of thought is involved in working out the way in which his account of the events is related to the grounds upon which it is based, for it is the coherence in the pattern of his thought that enables him to discern the systematic connection in the nature of things and yet it is only as he reaches that discernment that he is able to separate out the actual evidence upon which his account of the events must be allowed to rest. In so far as he can reduce to consistent and rational expression the ways in which his knowledge is related to the grounds upon which it is based, he is convinced that he has come to grips with the inherent rationality of things and is convinced of the truth of his reconstructions. Hence the crucial importance in many natural sciences of achieving wherever possible mathematical representation of our understanding of things, for it is in that way that we bring the objective rationality to view. Yet we may treat that representation only as an explicatory model or a disclosure model through which we interpretatively apprehend the reality we are investigating and not as a descriptive formula or as the equivalent of some ontic structure in the reality itself.

This scientific activity applies to the human sciences as well as the natural sciences, to historical or sociological science, for example; but it applies no less to theological science. In all of them, we are engaged properly in scientific activity only when we pass beyond description and narration to *explanation*, in which we penetrate, clarify, and explicate the inner intelligibility of what we investigate.

It is theological science viewed in this way that we are now to to consider, and in particular to think about three things:

(I) The distinctive nature and function of theological science, over against the other sciences, natural and social:

(II) the place of theology in the rapidly altering framework of scientific thought:

(III) the problem posed for theology by the split culture in which we find ourselves today.

I THE DIFFERENCE BETWEEN THEOLOGICAL SCIENCE AND THE OTHER SCIENCES

All the sciences are concerned to penetrate into the intelligible nature of things in their own fields and to bring it to coherent and convincing articulation. The natural and human sciences, however, operate only within the finite if unbounded universe, and thus within the limits of what is rationally accessible to us in nature. There are such limits, e.g. in physics set by the finite speed of light and the absolute zero of temperature. These sciences are concerned with developing the immanent rationalities of nature and are content to occupy themselves with fields of rationality that are not ultimately self-explanatory, refraining from asking the question as to the ultimate rational ground that lies behind every field of knowledge. These sciences must bracket themselves off from that kind of question in order to be what they are and to get on with their own task in exploring and understanding contingent happening. The theologian looks at this from a different angle and expresses it in a different way, but so far as the task of the natural scientist is concerned it amounts to the same thing. Since the universe has been created by God out of nothing, it has been given a contingent reality of its own, and must therefore be investigated in its contingent nature, and interpreted out of its own natural processes and created rationalities, and not out of God.

Theology, on the other hand, is the science that is unable to halt at the limits that must satisfy natural science, for it is concerned above all to penetrate into transcendent and fontal rationality, the ultimate source of all that is intelligible to man and which is presupposed in the created rationalities of nature explored through natural sciences. There is something analogous to this transcendent rationality in the transcendent element that presses itself upon us in every science. The passion of the scientist or the scholar is aroused by the intuitive apprehension of a reality that is not constructed or controlled by man but that waits to be discovered. And so he develops a science, the final shape of which does not lie within his own competence to determine. He glimpses its possibilities but they reach out far beyond him. As Michael Polanyi has put it, he is caught up in the pursuit of a reality that is only partially disclosed but that has an indeterminate range of rationality still unrevealed, for he is convinced that it has an independence and power for manifesting itself in unthought-of ways in the future.[1] His scientific conscience is the counterpart or echo in himself of that transcendent element, a logic beyond his own mind, that thrusts itself unrelentingly and compulsively upon him. That is why, as Polanyi has so often insisted, there can be no pure science pursued freely for its own sake without dedicated service to a transcendent rationality.[2] If there is to be real science

[1] See *Personal Knowledge* (Routledge and Kegan Paul, London, 1958), ch. 1 on 'Objectivity'.

[2] In *Science, Faith and Society* (O.U.P., 1946, and 1964 edit. with new Preface, The University of Chicago Press) or *The Tacit Dimension* (Routledge and Kegan Paul, London, 1967).

at all there must be cataleptic control of our human intellectual constructions by something that is itself not constructed, but received, a rationality that seizes us from above and beyond ourselves.

This transcendent element in the sciences of nature is not of course to be identified with God, for it comes at us out of the immanent rationality of nature, but it does cry aloud for God if only because the immanent rationality in nature does not provide us with any explanation of itself. The transcendent rationality of God, however, is ultimate and as such can be known only out of itself. If God really is God He confronts us with absolute priority. In the nature of the case, He can be known only on the free ground of His own self-subsistent Being and through the shining of His own uncreated Light. The Truth of God cannot be demonstrated from other ground or derive support from lesser truths for He is the ultimate ground and support of them all. That is why theology is often so baffling to those who are absorbed in the natural or human sciences with created or second-order rationalities which all require the support of one another, for in theological science we must presuppose the ultimate rationality into which we inquire in order to inquire rationally of God and we are unable to contend for Him on any lower ground than that which He is. It is all very well in the other sciences to bracket off the question as to ultimate rationality, that is, to be methodologically agnostic in understanding nature out of itself alone, but when we take away those brackets and ask the question as to ultimate rationality, to be agnostic would be an act of sheer irrationality, for it would mean that our reason was being loosed from its bond with the source of rational being. Conversely stated, knowledge of the ultimate rationality of God is reached at the point where our human reason becomes enlightened from beyond the limits of created rationality and where an infinite extension of intelligibility beyond ourselves is disclosed, but all this in such a way that the ultimate rationality sets up its law in the depth of our human rationality and is recognized and respected as the norm and source of our rational illumination. In this way the disclosure of God to us in His own ultimate rationality is at the same time the opening of our human mind in understanding of Him. But thus known, God is the most certain and compelling fact in all knowledge.

I have been speaking for the most part as if the rationality of God were passive and mute, but this is far from being the case. It is active divine *Logos*, the transcendent Word of God that strikes into the self-enclosed structures of human life and thought and opens them out to the infinite range of eternal reality, bearing upon us in such a way as to deliver us from the futility of ever falling back upon ourselves in the meaninglessness of man's monologue with himself or in the emptiness of nature in its final lack of self-explanation. What we do in theological science is to develop rational modes of inquiry appropriate to the transcendent Word of God, in which we seek to let God's own eloquent self-evidence sound through to us so that we may know and understand Him out of His own rationality and under the active determination of His divine being.

In the course of this activity we begin to understand something of how the cognitive relation of men to God can be so sharply refracted that double vision results in which human knowers are unable to trace the thought of God back to its proper ground in His reality, although they remain haunted, as it were, by the ultimate rationality of God all round them. This is where theological science must step in to help men refer their thoughts properly beyond themselves to God. In it we probe into the problematic condition of the human mind before God and seek to bring knowledge of Him into clear focus so that the Truth of God may shine through unhindered and the human mind may acquire clear and orderly forms through which to apprehend and conceive of His reality.

But it is here that *Christian dogmatics* is concerned with Jesus Christ as the One in whom the transcendent *Logos* of God is to be heard and identified, where we encounter the Truth of God in such a way that we ourselves are questioned down to the roots of our own being, where we are under unceasing attack from the side of ultimate reality, and where at last we can distinguish the Truth of God from ourselves and begin to ask the kind of question that does not shoot past God into emptiness and nothing, but really meets its target. Here we find ourselves up against the fundamental datum of God's self-revelation, as divine Word incarnate in our human existence, which takes our minds under its command in such a compelling and ultimate way that Jesus Christ gives decisive content and structure to our knowledge of God and constitutes the objective centre by reference to which Christian theology clarifies and develops its own inner dogmatics. In the terse words of Thomas Aquinas: *Christus qui secundum quod homo, via est nobis tendendi in Deum.*[1]

II THE RAPIDLY ALTERING FRAMEWORK OF SCIENTIFIC THOUGHT

What we must consider here is not simply the great transition of modern times from the Ptolemaic and Copernican systems of cosmology, but the change in which the frontiers of human thought are being pushed back beyond the limits of language, and the change in the nature and depth of objectivity that this involves.

It is not the task of the theologian to explore the physical universe as such, but he is after all a creature of space and time so that all his thinking, even about God, can take place only within space and time and the rational structures to which they give rise. I do not propose at the moment to discuss the problems for theology to which this gives rise,[2] but what I am concerned to do is to consider the way in which we make use of the framework of thought in space-time for our scientific penetration into the inner intelligibility of things, in nature or in God.

In Newtonian physics, space and time were regarded as constituting an inertial system and as playing an absolute role in the whole causal structure of science. Science of that kind operated with fundamental axioms that were placed at the beginning of a theory as formal premises and in the nature of the case could only develop closed theoretic systems. But with the advent of relativity theory, as I understand it, a great change takes place, for now the premises of science are not known or proven in advance but are known only *a posteriori*, and not apart from the whole process

---

[1] *Summa Theologica*, I. q. 2. Prol.
[2] See *Space, Time and Incarnation* (O.U.P., 1969).

of scientific inquiry, postulation and verification, and are accepted on the ground that they give intelligible and unifying form to the inferential relations in which they are incorporated. (It is a similar kind of structure that is exhibited in the axiomatic calculi of Russell's logic when modified by Gödel's theorem.) In other words, the axioms are not just a set of logical premises antecedent to and independent of the results reached, but arise out of the intrinsic connections of scientific activity, and force themselves upon us as the necessary structures of thought through which the intelligible nature of things imposes itself upon our minds. In this way, as Einstein used to point out, geometry applied to the physical universe ceases to be an axiomatic deductive science and becomes a natural science inseparably bound up with physics.[1] The axioms may indeed be formulated at first through postulation as we reflect on the way in which the facts are being established, but they have to be deductively tested (in Popper's sense), and are justified (in Polanyi's sense) in view of the objective depth and indeterminate range of rationality that becomes disclosed through them. The special point for us to note, however, is this: Here we have a rigorously scientific way of thought which is an axiomatic penetration into the inherent rationality of things beyond all our mental pictures of reality, a rationality that is itself not phenomenally or causally related to phenomena or empirical events and which could not be discerned merely from an observational or empirical approach, but which forces itself upon us as the rational ground lying behind phenomena or empirical events, and without which they could not be what they are.

I have spent some time in describing this, for this new way of axiomatic thinking in physics is very similar to the way in which we have come to operate in theology as we seek to penetrate into its inner logic, not by arguing logico-deductively from fixed premises but by laying bare the premises embedded in the intrinsic connections of the subject-matter. As examples of this in classical theology we may point to the *De incarnatione* of Athanasius or the

---

[1] See 'Geometry and Experience' in *Sidelights on Relativity* (Methuen, 1922), and 'Physics and Reality' (1936) in *Out of My Later Years* (Philosophical Library, New York, 1950).

Cur Deus homo? of Anselm. After the *sic et non* approach elaborated by Abelard, however, medieval theology took a different line. Reverting to the Aristotelian conception of science, it sought to reach necessary conclusions argumentatively derived from independently authoritative principles proper to the knowledge of God. Yet even then, as Aquinas pointed out, the procedure could not be purely logico-deductive since whenever we are concerned with being and reality, and objective and not merely conceptual implication must be discerned, we have to employ probable and persuasive argumentation, and not merely demonstrative reasoning in the relations of ideas, in order to compel the assent of faith and develop understanding. The fact that basic theological statements like 'God created the world' or 'The Son of God became a man' are contingent in nature forced Duns Scotus to question the reduction of theological science to the axiomatic pattern of Euclidean geometry all on one level. Nevertheless, scholastic theology with its fascination for logical analysis and syllogistic reasoning largely took shape as an axiomatic deductive science. From all this, however, and its strange revival in the Newtonian era, modern dogmatics, Roman and Protestant, has moved far away as attention was given to the interaction between God and historical existence in this world and therefore to the all-important relation between language and being, human and divine.

When our theological thinking cannot be detached from contingent events or empirical relations it must be controlled from beyond our minds by objective connections. Then we have to operate with premises that by their very nature cannot be anticipated by detached thought for they are discovered only as we let our thinking take shape under the determination of the reality into which we inquire and under the organic articulation of its inner structure and intelligibility. Premises or axioms of this kind have a surprising quality for they cannot be established antecedently, independently of empirical relation with reality, but become evident only in the adaptation of our reason to the transcendent element from which it derives its illumination. Pursued in this way theological dogmatics is, if you like, an axiomatic science in the new sense. Thus the statement 'God is love' cannot be treated as a timeless or necessary axiom, for then it would be uprooted from its ground in the self-revelation of God through the incarnation, detached from historical factuality in Jesus Christ, and abstracted from the operation of the divine love in His sacrifice, as if it were necessarily or universally true without reference to the activity in which God makes it true for us, and therefore apart altogether from the relevant question as to when and in what conditions this statement is true. That God is love is universally true for us; but it is not to be treated like a formal-logical premise for deductive operations, but only like the premises of science that are not known in advance but are known only *a posteriori* and therefore are not accepted apart from the whole pattern of scientific activity in the field in question.

It is natural that the dogmatic science of theology, in spite of the highly distinctive nature of its own subject-matter, should find somewhat congenial the altering framework of thought in the scientific world of today, and not least the way in which it works with thought-structures of a non-perceptual kind, demanding, as Dirac insisted, the exclusion of all mental pictures as distorting irrelevances.[1] It is through thought-structures of this kind derived from the biblical tradition that Judaeo-Christian theology penetrates behind man's childish fancies and observational abstractions to a knowledge of the indescribable and ineffable God. From this point of view alone the strange attempts of some modern thinkers to replace an out-dated 'image' of God by another 'image' deemed more suitable for the modern world, while still 'theologizing in pictures', appear quite retrograde and nonsensical.

There is, however, a problem in connection with the new mode of axiomatic thinking that must be faced. If we detach our premises from the static structure in which they are lodged on the Aristotelian or the Newtonian models, and, abandoning a point of absolute rest, choose a point of reference of our own by postulating some Archimedean point outside our earth-bound experience in order to come at the world from behind, do we not plunge into *relativism*? Many people in the modern world have

[1] The reference is taken from M. Polanyi, *Science, Faith and Society*, 1964 edit., p. 88.

seized on this idea with glee, as Hannah Arendt points out, in the belief that they have found a way of emancipating themselves from the shackles of spatiality and temporality and of achieving a godlike transcendence over nature.[1] But this is a fearful mistake, for relativism of this sort, far from liberating man, imprisons him within his own mental constructions and reduces all science in the last analysis to the science of the structures of man's own mind. Yet this gross delusion has bitten very deeply into our modern culture.

The real mistake lies behind all this—for relativity does not mean relativism. No doubt four-dimensional geometries have chanced into science through free postulatory thinking, but when it was found that they could and did in fact apply to actual existence, it was realized that they were not just ideal possibilities which the human mind happened to think up, but involved a far-reaching correlation between abstract conceptual systems and physical processes that carried us into an objective state of affairs beyond all our intuitive representations. Hence the dismantling by relativity theory of the old cosmologies and the kind of objectivities bound up with them, has brought to light a new and far profounder objectivity which is invariant with respect to our subjectivities. The epistemological implications of this are immense for all our thought, for by destroying the view that they are mere abstractions existing only in our human consciousness, it has demolished the old dualisms, whether in their Augustinian or Cartesian, Newtonian or Kantian forms, that have so adversely affected Western science and culture. Destroyed? Yes, perhaps so far as pure science is concerned, but alas they are still rampantly alive in our culture.

III THE PROBLEM OF OUR SPLIT CULTURE

Theologians, natural scientists, and social scientists are all at work side by side in the same world where their fields of inquiry inevitably overlap. They all develop their sciences in accordance

---

[1] *The Human Condition* (University of Chicago Press, 1958, Anchor Books edit., 1959), pp. 234ff. See also Karl Heim, *The Transformation of the Scientific World View* (S.C.M. Press, London, 1953), pp. 72ff.

with the state of knowledge at the time and in accordance with the relevant tools at their disposal, even though they have to refine and adapt them in the advance to new knowledge. They all aim at precise and controlled knowledge, knowledge within the structures of human thought and existence in space and time, and they seek to communicate understanding in the forms of thought and speech that arise within them. Hence they are committed, in some measure at least to the achievement of common understanding within the prevailing culture and to control through commonly-acknowledged explanation, without of course betraying what is distinctive in each science through false reductionism. But the fact remains that this culture of ours today is profoundly split from end to end. The line of the rift is not always straight, but it is particularly evident in the split between *pure science* and *social science*. Much has been written about the 'two cultures' to which I do not subscribe, but I cannot but feel that if such a split is allowed to become permanent it will result in the disintegration of civilization. Indeed it is already accountable for the widespread loss of meaning that afflicts our teenage and student population.

How does theology find itself in this situation today?

In order to answer that we must first see how the split has affected modern epistemology, in a sharp disjunction between *explanation* and *understanding*, i.e. between what Droysen (following Schleiermacher),[1] Dilthey, and Weber called *Erklären* and *Verstehen*. When they are split apart, however, each becomes distorted: explanation becomes severely restricted in its scope to what is clear-cut and amenable to logical processing, and is construed in terms of rigid causal and mechanical concepts instead of in terms of coherent and continuous patterns of structure and function; and understanding is construed as empathic interpretation, that is, the art of transposing oneself imaginatively and sympathetically into some situation in order to discern its distinctive qualities from within, instead of the grasping of discrete parts in a comprehensible whole through which we intuit reality in its

---

[1] Cf. Karl-Otto Apel, *Analytic Philosophy of Language and the Geisteswissenschaften* (Reidel, Dordrecht, 1967).

objective and intelligible relations. This results in the imprisonment of man in causal constructs on the one hand and in the social
objectifications of his own mental constructs on the other hand
—and it is certainly against both of these that students today are
constantly in revolt. Of course, attempts have been made and are
being made to reintegrate understanding and explanation as com-
plementary activities in scientific inquiry, e.g. the way in which
C. F. A. Pantin has brought together aesthetic recognition and
logical verification.[1] To my mind, some of the most successful
with respect to natural science are Michael Polanyi and Karl
Popper; different though they are, they are both committed to
objective interpretation in which explanation and understanding involve each other, although neither may be sufficiently empirical.
But the problem in natural science is not so acute as it is in social
science, where, as far as I can see, little success seems to result
from the attempts to introduce some real objectivity into empathic
methodologies by appealing to the universality of human behaviour and by linking them up to statistical science or linguistic
philosophy which are still bound up with the old particulate view
of nature that is a hang-over from the Newtonian era.[2] It would
seem to be the case that while the pure sciences, for the most part,
have overcome the Newtonian dualism between space and matter,
volume and mass, and have broken free from the rigid mechanistic concepts deriving from it, the social sciences are still deeply
infected with dualist and instrumentalist notions of science, and
have yet to develop within their own fields the kind of connection
that comes to view in field theory, although this is readily open
to 'understanding' as we let our knowledge of things and events
in their own states be illuminated by the intelligible relations
directly forced on our recognition by the things and events themselves. It is difficult to see how we can heal the disastrous breach
between explanation and understanding until we leave behind the
obsolete dualism that lies at the source of it.

[1] *The Relations between the Sciences*, edit. by A. M. Pantin and W. H. Thorpe
(Cambridge U.P., 1968), ch. 5, pp. 100ff.

[2] Cf. P. Winch, *The Idea of a Social Science and its Relation to Philosophy* (Routledge and Kegan Paul, London, 1958); R. S. Rudner, *Philosophy of Social Science*
(Prentice-Hall, Englewood Cliffs, N.J., 1966).

Now all human thought develops with language; but since language can exist only in a society, our thought is inescapably bound up with the institutions and patterns and traditions of the community in which we live and work. That is why even our most refined concepts are psychologically and socially conditioned. But if the culture of our society is so deeply split even at the basic points of explanation and understanding, it is not surprising that all our scientific activity is affected, e.g. in the deep tensions between pure science and socially-controlled technology. That applies not least to theology, if only because of the deep interconnection between Church and society. If no science can advance to radically new knowledge without a real struggle against the linguistic and conceptual 'paradigms' of the community, as Thomas S. Kuhn has called them,[1] then the tension is at its greatest in those sciences which, like theology, are so firmly set in social existence.

That is the problem of the split culture for modern theology, but let us consider how it has been affected only at two points.

(a) In the distorting disjunction between explanation through rigid mechanico-causal connections and understanding through empathic participation or interiorized observation, many theologians have suffered from what Martin Buber has designated a 'conceptual letting go of God'.[2] That was early apparent in Schleiermacher's refusal to think of God as the object of our conceiving and knowing on the ground that He cannot be exposed to our 'counter-influence', i.e. the objectifying force of our active reason, but insisted that we may understand Him in so far as He is for us simply 'the co-determinant' of our feeling of absolute dependence.[3] Behind that of course lay a radical dichotomy between 'the sensuous' and 'the spiritual', the given and the not-given, which had the effect of throwing him back upon the emotions of the religious self-consciousness and reducing theological propositions to accounts of 'religious affections set forth in speech'.

[1] *The Structure of Scientific Revolutions* (University of Chicago Press, Phoenix edit., 1964), ch. 5, pp. 43ff.
[2] *The Eclipse of God* (Harper, New York, 1957), pp. 123-5.
[3] *The Christian Faith* (T. and T. Clark, Edinburgh, 1928), p. 17f.

A similar approach appears even in the highly rationalistic theology of Paul Tillich for whom the 'direct object' of theology was 'not God' but what he called 'religious symbols' which mediated not objective content but power.[1] Correspondingly Tillich held that faith is essentially 'non-conceptual', so that it can yield theology only if it borrows rational structures from something else and is conceptualized through them. Again, the same kind of thinking is to be found in those Continental theologies which have succumbed to the existentialist flight from science and have cut themselves loose from all objectivity, for they are unable to distinguish genuine objectivity from the objectivist structures emanating from absolute and static notions of space and time. In other words, the dichotomy between explanation and understanding cuts man off from cognitive relation to God and throws him back upon his own self-understanding, with the result that relations with God and relations with the world tend to be reduced in the last analysis to relations between man and himself. And because this is fostered by the deep split in our culture and the present state of social science, it is not surprising that some theologians in this country seem to lose their nerve, and lapse from theology and the philosophy of theology into the phenomenology and sociology of religion. There is certainly a place for the phenomenology and sociology of religion when they are not distorted through damaged notions of understanding and explanation, but even in their sound form they cannot be allowed to take the place of scientific and philosophical theology.

There seems little doubt that in all this 'conceptual letting go of God' the real problem is not a conflict between science and theology but the conflict between what Santillana has called 'a philosophy of order and design' on the one hand and 'romantic naturalism' on the other hand.[2]

(b) Even more striking is the way in which New Testament and historical studies have been caught in the toils of the split culture. The story here also goes back to Newton. The fact that time was

---

[1] 'Theology and Symbolism' in *Religious Symbols*, edit. by F. E. Johnson (Harper, New York, 1955), p. 108.
[2] *The Origins of Scientific Thought* (University of Chicago Press, 1961), p. 301.

associated by Newton with space in the fundamental structure of knowledge meant that spatial extension in time and therefore history entered fully into the arena of scientific study. The effect of this, however, was paradoxical. Because time was inseparably bound up with space in conditioning matters of fact, the linear character of history, and thus the proleptic, predictive trend of events, had to be taken seriously. But because time and space were given an absolute status in a homogeneous and undifferentiated system, a static and necessary quality was imported into the notion of history. There we have seeds of the fatal division between two kinds of history. But that developed only after English deism cross-fertilized with the radical dualisms in German thought, the Platonic-Augustinian dualism between the intelligible and sensible realms that was latent in Lutheran theology, not least in its schematic distinction between 'the two kingdoms', the Cartesian dualism between subject and object, and the Greek antithesis between idea and event that was revived through the Kantian distinction between noumenal 'things in themselves' and phenomenal 'things for us'. Then there appeared 'the ugly big ditch', as Lessing called it, between the necessary truths of reason and the accidental truths of history. Are we to leap across that ditch from the accidental truths of history into a different kind of truth altogether, leaving history discarded as the external symbolic wrapping of timeless truth? As German thinking developed, the divergence became more systematic. Actual history came to be left to the tender mercies of positivist science after the fashion of Mill or Comte, which insisted that historical processes should be observed, explained, and established through methods assimilated to the empirico-causal method of natural science on the Newtonian model. On the other hand, history came to be regarded as 'objectified life', the deposit of what Hegel called 'objectified mind', or the creative objectifications of man's self-understanding, which as such had to be interpreted through methods correlated with the human subject, i.e. understanding, empathic divination or participation in its inner form. This distinction has been reinforced through the development of phenomenology in such a way that the split between explanation and understanding, cause and meaning, has resulted in two quite different notions of history, called (since Herrmann and Troeltsch) *Historie* and *Geschichte*.

One kind, denoted by *Historie*, was applied to the New Testament to get rid of everything that did not fit in with the rigid structures of a mechanistic interpretation of the universe as a closed continuum of cause and effect. The other kind, denoted by *Geschichte*, was applied to the New Testament in order to make it the great text for man's understanding of himself cut off alike from his conceptual relation to God and from his conceptual relation to nature. It is hardly surprising that methods of New Testament criticism operating with these radical dichotomies, which (in D. M. MacKinnon's words) 'translate propositions concerning actual historical transactions into propositions relating to the spiritual and religious activities of individuals and groups', only succeed in reducing the historical Jesus Christ to a vanishing-point. But what follows from this, as MacKinnon argues, is 'an anthropocentrism in theology that could be criticized as a most dangerous species of mythological illusion'.[1] To say the least, however, such an approach to Jesus that thrusts man back through encounter with himself upon his own mental structures divorced from objective and explanatory control from beyond himself is the antithesis of the unremitting attack of Jesus upon every form of human self-centredness.

It is obviously very difficult for theologians who are concerned with the advance of dogmatic science in the rigorous sense to accept the 'results' of these strange operations in the interpretation of the New Testament, for the end-products are predetermined by the highly questionable assumptions with which the scholars concerned have gone to work. The divorce of understanding from explanation shuts the interpreter up to two alternatives. In one, he detaches biblical language from its natural, direct intention, and isolates its 'oblique intention' as the primary carrier of its meaning which must then be 'understood' in terms of the attitudes or forms of life or decisions which it evokes. In the other, he isolates the syntactical meaning of biblical statements and subjects it to 'scientific' treatment through an analysis of the morphological

[1] *Borderlands of Theology* (Lutterworth Press, London, 1968), p. 88.

linguistic connections in which it is intrinsically carried, and 'understands' it in terms of the use to which it is put in specific contexts. Attempts are now being made to bring these together. The second alternative is brought in to heal the former of the arbitrary character given it through 'understanding' which can operate through *any* empathic relation and so precludes the possibility of proper verification. The first alternative is brought in to redeem the second from the sterility imparted to it in the substitution of the analysis of statements for the analysis of facts and events, by helping it to treat language as forms of life capable of behavioural and social meaning to be 'understood' through correlation with life situations. The fact remains, however, that both these alternatives fall on one and the same side of the cultural split where they are cut off from the referential and significatory function of language and so can proceed only by abstracting from reality, and only appear to engage in explanation when some sort of mental existence is posited in place of reality and a false ontology develops which can lend colour to the claim to objective verification and control. Only when we overcome the split in our culture can we engage in an interpretation that penetrates inductively into the genuine intelligibility of facts or the coherent reasons of things through explanatory axioms or premises which give unity and objective depth to the understanding. It is theological hermeneutic or 'depth-exegesis' (as William Manson used to call it) of this kind that is desperately needed in order to deliver biblical scholarship from its dependence on the subjectivity of the interpreters and their unverifiable methods. But so long as the cultural split continues, the passage from language to reality is obstructed, so that interpretation can take only two mutually exclusive forms in which 'causes' and 'meanings', 'realities' and 'signs', are set over against each other to their common detriment and distortion, resulting in some form of positivism or romanticism.

Yes, modern theological studies are certainly struggling in the toils of our split culture. But there is quite another side to the story. Wherever theology is being pursued rigorously as a dogmatic science in ecumenical dialogue across the Churches and in dialogue with the other sciences and with the philosophy of science, it becomes purified of pseudo-theological structures that have obtruded into it from the distorting subjectivities of our split culture, and achieves a new depth and unity that cut across the ancient barriers of Church and Church, and of Church and Israel, in a quite astonishing way. Through the unification and simplification that arises in this way, theology is now engaged in one of the most significant advances in all its long history.

5

Ecumenism and Science[1]

Ecumenical activity takes place within the space and time of this world. It is the world that came into being out of nothing through the creative Word of God, while space and time arose as functions of contingent events within the creation and as bearers of its immanent order. It was in this world that God placed man, and within its space and time that He has made Himself known. Man was appointed to live in the world and enjoy it, endowed with skills to know and name it, to occupy it and have dominion over it, and thus as the crown of creation to be its priest through whom the response of all creatures might be made articulate in the praise and worship of the Creator. This is also the world into which God sent His Son, the Word made flesh, to reveal the love of the Father, to overcome the estrangement into which the world had fallen and to deliver it from its futility, so that the communion of man with God and the purpose of God for man within the creation might be renewed. Thus not only has God created the world out of nothing, with space and time as the medium of its order and of His interaction with nature, but He has confirmed it and established its relation to Himself through the incarnation of His Son within it, at once affirming the reality of space and time for the fulfilment of His own eternal purpose and binding man to space and time as the sphere of his life and work and communion with the Father.

This is the world of space and time in which man in obedience to the Creator is engaged in exploring the order of created existence and bringing its rational beauty to articulation in natural and

[1] Prepared for the *Centre d'Études Oecumeniques*, Strasbourg, June, 1968.

theoretic science, and in which the Church in obedience to the Saviour is engaged in the mission of reunion, proclaiming the Word of reconciliation and living it out among men, through evangelism and ecumenism. The community of science and the Church of Jesus Christ are at work side by side in the same world, seeking understanding within the structures of space and time and seeking to communicate understanding in the forms of human thought and speech that arise within them. It is in this world of concrete actualities in nature and history accessible to man's observation and reflection that the Church pursues its theological task, for it is not apart from them that God has made Himself known and it must be within them that theology fulfils its scientific function of clarification and explanation. But these actualities of nature and history are also those which natural science investigates and seeks to explain by laying bare their immanent rational connections. Theological science and natural science both operate within the realm of human inquiry and both have to let their thinking serve the realities into which they inquire. Each has its own specific concern to take up, its own special modes of rationality and verification determined for it by the nature of its object, and scientific rigour requires those *differentia* to be unquestioningly respected, but both have the same basic problems of knowledge, in conforming knowing to the nature of reality, in distinguishing knowing from what is known, and in reflecting self-critically upon their own scientific operations. Since in neither case can science detach itself from the humanity that is involved in it, cutting off knowledge of the object from the fact that it is knowledge by a human subject, and since in each case it is only too easy for us to impose masterful forms of thought upon the realities we seek to investigate, we must constantly engage in acts of fundamental reorientation in which our concepts and terms are matched with their material content. Moreover, since scientific explanation involves an understanding which we can communicate to others and bring them to accept, we are committed to the achievement of common understanding and to control through commonly acknowledged explanation.

All this makes it quite impossible to separate ecumenism and science in watertight compartments, for while a responsible ecumenical theology must be concerned with its own proper object, and only within the bounds imposed by that object take up the problems and questions posed by the sciences, it must seek to articulate and unify its knowledge within the same realm of thinking that is occupied by every other science. Certainly in our day, theology can be pursued only in a world that is dominated by empirical science and conditioned from end to end by the effects of its application in technology, but far from meaning that it must let its own material content or its results be determined by any other science, this means that theology is forced to pursue its own activity in a more scientifically rigorous and disciplined way on its own ground and in accordance with the nature of its own proper object. Dialogue between theology and the other sciences is a searching and purifying experience, for it exposes the foreign elements that have obtruded into it and questions the pseudo-theological structures to which they have given rise, but this can only serve the consolidation and unification of knowledge for which a scientific theology is bound to work—and that is the basic contribution it can and ought to make to ecumenism. What we are concerned with here, then, is not the contribution of the other sciences in any way to the material content of ecumenism, but with the ecumenical results that accrue from rigorous scientific thinking within theology.

It may help before we go further to think a little of what we intend by *science*. Science is nothing more or less than clear, precise knowledge. Neither in natural science nor in Christian theology do we have an esoteric way of knowing. There is only one basic way of human knowing which is found to operate in every field of human experience, in religious as well as natural knowledge. Science is the rigorous and disciplined extension of that basic way of knowing applied in exact, controlled, and organized ways to different fields of experience. In every field we know something in accordance with its nature, and so we let its nature determine for us the mode of rationality we must adopt toward it and the form of learning or discovery appropriate to it. If the nature of what we seek to know is quite determinate and mute, then we must act accordingly, and put our questions in a determinate, experimental form in which we force it to answer us and so to declare itself to us. That is what we do in physics. But if the nature of what we seek to know is self-determining and capable of self-expression, then we must act accordingly, and put our questions in a different empirical form in which we listen to what it has to say to us in its own self-disclosure. That is what we do in psychology. The same fundamental mode of knowing is adopted in each case, but science requires us to take into account the difference in the nature of the object and to allow our knowing to take a course appropriate to it. We cannot prescribe in advance how anything is to be known but allow what we learn of its nature, as we proceed, to modify and adapt our mode of learning and discovery. This applies equally to our knowledge of God. It would be scientifically impossible to prescribe toward Him the same kind of approach which obtains in physics or in psychology, for that would be to presuppose from the start that God is not different from what we investigate in those sciences. If He is not a physical object we cannot manipulate Him by experimental questioning and if He is not a dumb idol we cannot put our own answers into His mouth, but must rather adopt in our inquiry of Him the kind of approach that obtains in prayer and listen for His Word. In our inquiry into natural processes we are concerned with *discovery*, but in our inquiry into God's activities we are concerned with *revelation*: that is in line with the scientific requirement to develop knowledge strictly in accordance with the nature of that into which we inquire.

Scientific knowledge of this kind implies that we must learn to distinguish what we know from our subjective states and conditions. This is one way to state the basic scientific principle of *objectivity*, but it is only an extension of our fundamental mode of rationality. We are rational when we act in accordance with the nature of the object. To behave as though this table were not there or as though it were a personal being would be quite irrational, for it would not be treating what is 'there' in terms of what is the case. Since scientific thinking rejects all irrationality and unreality of this sort it will not allow us to impose upon any object we claim to know ideas of our own invention or ideas that we have transferred to it from some other kind of thing. This is why the scientific thinker must be ruthlessly critical of himself and his preconceptions, in order to prevent himself from overlaying the object of his knowledge with stuff that does not belong to it and which only obscures and distorts genuine knowledge of it.

On the other hand, since we must let the nature of what we know prescribe for us the mode of rationality we adopt toward it, science must take account of the subject of the human knower. In fact it requires of us, with all its rigour, controlled adaptation of the subject to the object. That is why it is quite unscientific to transfer from one field to another the distinctive mode of rationality that develops within it. Thus we cannot assume impersonal, objectivist forms of behaviour toward personal subjects, but must assume personal, objective modes of behaviour toward them if we are to know them in a responsible and rational way. This is why it would be quite nonsensical to look for God through a radar telescope or to imagine that we can reduce knowledge of Him to a mathematical formula. Here we are up against the scientific principle of *fidelity* which lies at the bottom of what we call 'the scientific conscience'. We must be faithful to what we know, and act and think in ways of relentless fidelity toward it. Of course this will take an appropriate form in natural science according to the processes or phenomena under investigation and another form in theological science where the human reason suffers an adaptation in accordance with God's self-revealing activity and nature. Hence what Christians call 'faith' is not something irrational, far less anti-rational, but precisely the very opposite, the proper behaviour of the reason in accordance with the nature of the divine Object, i.e. rational love. Something of this is apparent in our personal ethical relations with others in which we learn to love our neighbour objectively for his sake, no less than we love ourselves, and in which we ourselves attain richer and fuller subjectivity. But it is supremely in rational love toward God, as we love Him objectively for His sake who is the source of all love and rationality, that we ourselves are established as rational human subjects. This is objectively orientated and controlled subjectivity, the faith that works by love, that faith in which the human reason freed from self-love is open and ready for the truth.

The application of this scientific thinking to ecumenism has a critical as well as a constructive effect. By the precision of its instruments it cuts through our common and traditional thought down to the roots of our concepts, clearing away the confusion that comes from the admixture of false subjectivity, and discriminating between apposite and inapposite forms of thought. It breaks up the rigidities of traditional language so that the realities they intend can shine through them once more, and opens out the processes of formalization so that religious patterns may be apprehended as the clues to what lies beyond them and be reconstructed in the light of what becomes progressively revealed. But science does more than attack and overcome the destructive tendencies at work in the human mind. By purging and refining the relations of our thought to being, it serves the imposition upon the mind of real and objective connections in things and develops the basic structures upon which the whole edifice of thought may be safely and consistently erected. This can be achieved in theology only through tension with popular religious consciousness as well as naturalistic existence, but it imports both an analytic simplicity and an enlightening synthesis which compel assent and build agreement.

In considering the place and function of scientific criticism, we must recall that human thought arises and grows only within the profound interconnection between language and society. Through human language thinking is inescapably bound up with the institutions, patterns, and traditions of the communities in which we live—that is why even the most refined scientific concepts are psychologically and socially conditioned. This sets the arena for a host of problems for the community of science and for the Christian Church, but it is worth contrasting the procedure that natural science adopts in dealing with them and the procedure commonly found in modern theology.

In the process of scientific inquiry the questions themselves must be constantly questioned in order to free them from distortion emanating from the side of the questioner, but that means that the questioning must cut back into the built-in habits of the questioning self and the structure of life, society, and language in which it is rooted. Thus whenever natural science engages in heuristic acts which require the formation of new concepts and terms it is forced to struggle with the patterns and rigidities of the community mind in order to free its thinking for the assimilating of what is really new; but in so far as it succeeds in transcending the hardening formalization and self-entrenchment of society it is able to serve and advance its true ends. A different procedure, however, tends to develop in theology, in connection with the mission of the Church to communicate its message to the common man —this has been particularly evident in Protestant theology since the nineteenth century. In this procedure, theology is translated into the language and thought-forms of the people and the culture of the day, with the result that it suffers from the backward drag of popular religion and the ideological twist of the prevailing social consciousness. Thus the theology of the Church is tempted to become the servant of public opinion; but since popular thought tends to be a sedimentary deposit within our naturalistic existence of outworn scientific ideas, theology through this procedure acquires a built-in obsolescence. There can be no doubt that this makes ecumenical activity a very difficult and complicated process, for it has to reckon with deeply rooted non-theological factors embedded in the religious, ecclesiastical and theological patterns of the different Churches, but it does mean that if ecumenical activity is to succeed it must involve a movement of renewal in social as well as theological patterns.

Scientific theology thus becomes a *sine qua non* of ecumenism in which we come to grips with the psychological and sociological conditioning even of our most profound theological concepts. In theological science as in natural science, to think precisely and to advance to new levels of understanding require progressive logical reconstruction of society and such an engagement with the truth that it makes us free from the untruth and unreality in ourselves. But this can only serve the essence of the Gospel in the call of Christ to renounce ourselves, take up the cross, and follow Him.

Scientific questioning reinforces the evangelical demand for repentance or *metanoia*, that is for an alteration in the basic structure of our mind. Our greatest difficulty lies in the human self and its inherent selfishness for it is that which distorts scientific and theological questioning *ab initio*, and infects the answers to our questions with their ideological twist. If the Church is the community of those who are emancipated by the truth of Christ, and who are redeemed by His power from sin and self-will and therefore from imprisonment in the self-centred and arbitrary preconceptions of the self, then the adoption of rigorous scientific procedures in ecumenism must serve the evangelical edification and renewal of the Church. Moreover, since the Christian Gospel is the supreme enemy of all selfishness and self-centredness, it ought to contribute to the struggle of all pure science for objectivity, in freedom from false subjectivity.

Christian theology, however, has a more complicated problem with which to cope than natural science has. On the one hand, its essential concern makes it give the human subject a fuller and more integral place in knowledge and community, but for that reason its must penetrate down to the ingrained selfishness of man at a deeper level, in its character as sin, in enmity to God and refusal of charity to others. Yet no more than preaching can theology do that without at the same time provoking the resistance of human self-will into the erection of defence-mechanisms against the attack of the Gospel. On the other hand, it is concerned with religious symbolisms that are more closely bound up with the life and behaviour of the self and society than are the abstract symbolisms of natural science; but these religious symbolisms for that reason are easily infected by man's sinful self-centredness and become quickly deployed in its defence-mechanisms. This is why sin is found to be at work in the subtlest and profoundest ways in religious forms.

Psychologically, the problems are not different from those with which we have to do elsewhere, in the social sciences, for example, or even in logic.[1] In the primary symbolism which we use,

---

[1] See the illuminating discussions of E. H. Hutten in *The Origins of Science*, chs. xiii–xiv.

language, it is evident that the development of verbal signs and of understanding proceeds as one, for we require language as the instrument with which to grasp things and present them to ourselves for consideration, thus achieving on our part transcendence over them, the rationality of acting in accordance with what is not ourselves, and advance in knowledge. Symbolism involves a distinction between the sign and what is signified, and thus represents the distinction between our knowing and what we know, what we say and what we speak about. We use signs, therefore, to attend away from ourselves in acts of semantic reference, and it is in that objective reference that they have their justification. Rightly related to what they signify, signs are transparent media absolutely essential for life and knowledge. When that relation is damaged everything becomes opaque and obscure and we tend to explain or find meaning in things not through transcendent reference away from ourselves but in terms of our own inner world, but then our symbolism becomes geared into our inherent self-centredness and is made into the vehicle of our subjective states and desires. If the schism between symbols and that to which they originally referred arises, as psychologists tell us, under the pressure of unconscious drives, such as the upsurge of anxiety, it is maintained and exploited by the in-turned self for its own ends. Whenever this happens there tends to take place a further division within the symbol itself, between the outer form and the inner mental content; but when the inner content becomes that to which the symbol refers it is treated as some sort of mental existence. And so there develops a false ontology which hardens the original distinction between symbol and objective reality into a serious rift, and reveals a schizoid disjunction between ideas and events. Undoubtedly, the formalization of our knowledge in signs or symbols is necessary for every advance in knowledge to higher levels of understanding, but when they become quite detached from their original reference, they lose their control and become arbitrary, and instead of advance there can only take place a lapse back into the circle of our own subjectivity.

A movement of this kind is evident in recent phenomenological and form-critical approach to the New Testament, with its sharp bifurcation between *Geschichte* and *Historie*, together with its treatment of literary forms as referring to the world of mental existence in the Early Church, for behind it there lies the familiar schizoid disjunction between ideas and history with its usual accompaniments of substitute-symbolism and substitute-ontology. But it is very important to see that this sort of thing is apt to be rife wherever we are concerned with *religious* symbolism, that is, where symbols and signs operate in the relation between man and God which has been damaged by sin, and reconciliation in being and knowing is desperately needed. In this realm where not only the law but every kind of formalization can become the strength of sin, the in-turned self of man makes use of religious symbolism in the development of his defence-mechanisms behind which he takes refuge, entrenched in his own self-justifying activity. In these circumstances religious symbolism becomes the powerful carrier of our naturalistic fantasies and the means through which even our most carefully refined theological concepts are corrupted and twisted round to mean something quite different from what their original formulation intended. As an example of this, we may point to the difference between Luther's *pro me* and Bultmann's *pro me*, together with the change in the understanding of justification by faith found in modern Protestantism, that is, from justification by grace as the objective act of Christ on our behalf and apart from us, to justifying faith interpreted to modern man in terms of his own existential decision detached from any objective act of Christ in history.

These psychological mechanisms masquerading in religious and ecclesiastical symbolisms are everywhere evident in the ecumenical movement as Churches confront Churches and especially as they try to work out ways of actual reunion. It does not take much by way of scientific sociological research to show that the grounds for disunity between them and the reasons for remaining apart are more non-theological than theological, at least as far as the Evangelical Churches are concerned. The principle *cuius regio, eius religio* still maintains its power. This is certainly evident in Scotland where the ecumenical spirit has obviously brought to the surface age-old fantasies embedded in religious and ecclesiastical symbolisms, and where it becomes clearer every day that the real obstacle to reunion is nationalistic egoism. This has been fanned into a flame by popular music, art and literature that are deeply infected with romantic naturalism and are concerned with self-expression and self-fulfilment as the criteria of significance. Among teenagers, of course, this has contributed to the problem of stuck-adolescence and has even led to a marked regression to infantile behaviour. But in the Church itself it has brought about a state of affairs in which it is difficult to communicate or to engage in dialogue except within the orbit of the religious self-expression of the Scottish people and its 'genius'. This has inevitably meant a return to the old womb from which came the historic bitternesses and divisions and a lapse into rigid and closed systems of thought such as one finds in paranoiacs as well as infants. The same psychopathology is also apparent in sections of the Press where a deliberate campaign has been mounted for several years to create trouble and tension, accompanied by claims that all this is the direct, deleterious result of the ecumenical movement, which reminds us of the twisted behaviour of the paranoid patient who provokes events to justify his claim that he is being victimized. But it is no less evident in theological publications such as the notorious book, *Power without Glory*,[1] by the late Professor Ian Henderson of Glasgow, in which a violent attack upon Ecumenism is launched under repeated protests of Christian love, but which is quite unable to conceal intense obsessional hatred of the English. The Presbyterian symbolisms which he invokes have become the carriers of his own fantasies, for they have clearly been split off from their original ground in Reformed theology. It is significant that Henderson fully shares both Bultmann's schizoid attitude to the historical Jesus and his desperate anxieties lest the ecumenical movement should lead to a revival of Nicene theology. All this calls aloud for detailed examination and precise scientific thinking in ecumenical discussion, and for the development of an ecumenical theology into which there are built self-correcting devices enabling us to disentangle pure theology from the impurities of our own subjective states and desires.

Hutchinson, London, 1967.

But what of the alien concepts that have been allowed to obtrude into theological structures impertinently from other areas of knowledge and which have created false problems within the Church? Here we are concerned not so much with psychological as with epistemological analysis in order to test the forms of thought and speech we employ to see whether they match the proper content of theology and have arisen on the ground of actual knowledge of God. This is the area of scientific thinking in theology where we seek to clarify the rational structures of thought in space and time, where the same concepts and terms are employed by other sciences, but where there must take place in each a radical shift in meaning corresponding to its specific intention. Thus in the nature of the case there cannot be a one-to-one correspondence between the same terms in the various sciences, far less between the same terms in theological and natural science, although some form of real co-ordination is necessary unless theological concepts are to be cut adrift altogether from the structures of space and time in which God has placed us and through which He has made Himself known to us.

Let us consider the concept of *space* itself which has very far-reaching implications. The Early Church found that they had to come to terms with the problem of space soon after the Gospel began to be expounded within the world of Greek culture and science, in which some form of the receptacle idea predominated. In its Aristotelian form this was the notion of space as delimited place defined in terms of a containing vessel and with reference to a centre of immobility. Since anything beyond determinate space was unthinkable and unintelligible, it implied that if God is intelligible He must be finite. This was impossible for Christian theology since God is the transcendent Source of all rationality and has absolute priority over all space and time. The doctrine of the creation of the universe out of nothing meant that while space and time arise in and with the creation, they are made by God to be the bearers of its order; and the doctrine of the incarnation, according to which the Son of God has entered into our world of space and time to be one with us, meant that God interacts with our world of human and natural existence in such a way as to assert the reality of space and time for God in His relations with us and to bind us to space and time in all our relations with Him. Patristic theology rejected the notion of space or place as some kind of vessel and developed instead a relational and differential concept of space as the seat of relations or the place of meeting and activity in the interaction between God and the world. It was a distinctively theological understanding of space not tied down to any particular cosmology. Medieval theology in the West, however, took over the receptacle view of space in its most difficult Aristotelian form and in one way or another this has dominated the history of thought until modern times. The form of the receptacle notion of space which emerged out of the Renaissance in the thought of Galileo and Gassendi was further elaborated and firmly built into the structure of Western thought in Newtonian science, until it had finally to give way before the space-time of relativity theory, but its integration into theological thought produced a host of difficulties that are still with us. Historical and epistemological analysis shows this to be a foreign concept wrongly grafted into Christian doctrine with serious consequences in the divisions of the Church because of the pseudo-theological structures to which it gave rise. We will be able to glance only at several of these.

Somehow Latin Christianity took over the idea of the receptacle very early and allowed it to play a considerable role in the development of its doctrines of Church, Sacraments, and Order. This was closely allied to the notion of 'means of grace' not found in the East. In the history of Augustinian theology supernatural grace came to be thought of as contained in ecclesiastical vessels and capable of being handed on in space and time by means of them. This was given more definite formulation in the development of Canon Law. We shall consider the question of Orders later, but at this point it may be noted that the receptacle idea contributed deeply to a difference between East and West in regard to the doctrine of the Church as the Body of Christ. Whereas the Greek Fathers declined to think of the Church as the containing place of the Spirit but rather of the Church as possessed by the Spirit, the Latin Fathers tended to think of the Spirit as animating the body of the Church and of the Church as containing and possessing the Spirit of Christ much as in popular thought the body was thought of as the container or prison-house of the soul. This affected also the way in which Western thought construed the idea that the Church is the Ark of Salvation with its *extra ecclesiam nulla salus*. It is at these points that we see the profound divergence between East and West in the whole approach to *Catholicity* which was more rigidly and exclusively conceived in the West through being tied to the corporate institution of the visible Church, with the result that the Spirit of God came to be regarded as the Soul of the Church. Care has clearly been taken to oust this Augustinian idea from Roman doctrine in the constitution *De Ecclesia* of *Vaticanum II*, so that at long last there emerges at this very point the chance for rapprochement between Orthodox and Roman theology.

The difficulty became more sharply focused in the adoption of Aristotelian thought in Medieval theology, with its definition of place as the *terminus continentis immobilis primus* related to a centre of absolute rest in the earth and in the unmoved Mover beyond it. This led the Medievals to think of the presence of God almost entirely in a spatial manner, apart from time, which affected its cosmology and its whole outlook on history no less than its eschatology. But since according to Aristotle there is a relation of interdependence between the containing vessel and what it contains this idea of space implied a cataphatic conceptual control over whatever is conceived by means of it. This not only forced the West to differ from the East in regard to the mode of the *real presence* of Christ in the Eucharist but created insuperable difficulties within the orbit of Western theology, forcing Thomists and Occamists alike to resort to quite artificial distinctions in order to account for the fact that the body of Christ is present in the whole host, in each part of it, and in a multitude of hosts at the same time, without any commensurable relation between His body and the space of the place in which it is contained. Transubstantiation itself was contrary to the substance-accidents schema of Aristotelian thought, although it was clearly an attempt to break loose from it.

In the Reformation, Lutheran theology took over quite uncritically the receptacle notion of space from Occamist thought both in its doctrine of the real presence and in its Christology. Although it was not followed here by Reformed or Anglican thought, it is certainly Lutheran theology that has dominated the Protestant scene with the result that it extrapolated into it the same basic problems that we find in the late Medieval world. These were greatly accentuated when Lutheran thought was cross-fertilized by Newtonian thought which also operated with a receptacle view of space, and when the English deism that arose out of Newtonian thought infected Germany and contributed so much to the deadly dualism that has ever since characterized German philosophy and theology alike. The Church-dividing consequences of the receptacle idea were apparent from the start in the sharp conflicts between the Lutheran and the Reformed. The receptacle notion of space was extremely important for Luther for it was his way of asserting the reality and actuality of the Son of God in our human and earthly existence, and so he concentrated with a furious intensity upon the fact that the whole Son or Word of God is contained in the infant of Bethlehem and communicated to us in the sacrament of the Lord's Supper. That was for him the all-important ontological bridge between the two Kingdoms. But when Reformed theologians returned to the Patristic mode of speaking of the Son of God in the incarnation as having descended from heaven without abandoning His government of the universe, Lutherans operating only with a receptacle notion of space could only interpret this to mean that in the incarnation something of the Son or Word of God was left 'outside' (*extra*)—hence the so-called *extra Calvinisticum*. There was no doubt much confusion on both sides of these controversies, with considerable terminological imprecision; but when Reformed theologians spoke of the ascension of Christ above the heaven of heavens, beyond the created universe to the right hand of the Father, transcending all our conceptions of space and time, and yet spoke of the location of Christ's body in heaven, they were again trying to reject the receptacle notion of space while insisting that in His ascension the body of Christ did not lose its creaturely character or reality as a human body. It was their intention to make clear that as the incarnation meant the entry of the Son into space and time without the loss of God's transcendence over space and time, so the ascension meant the transcendence of the Son over space and time without the loss of His incarnational involvement in the dimensionalities of space and time. Lutherans, however, were unable to follow them in this way of speaking and could only read Reformed statements about the body of Christ in heaven to mean that it was confined there as in a container in the way they conceived of the incarnational presence of Christ in the body. Again when Reformed theologians tried to expound the real presence of Christ in the Eucharist but because of the Ascension distinguished it from the real presence of Christ at the Last Day, they rejected the receptacle notion of space which cut off spatial from temporal relation, and insisted in understanding the Eucharistic *parousia* as the active self-presentation of Christ to us in temporal as well as spatial extension, which reaches out toward the consummation in the final *parousia*. Lutherans were unwilling to consider this, since from their point of view it appeared to detract from the full actuality of the real presence of Christ in the Sacrament, yet they could maintain their view only at the expense of making the real presence timeless, i.e. a purely spatial presence unconditioned by time. But since spatial presence apart from time was difficult also for the Lutherans, they relied on the notion of the mathematical point to help them over the difficulty. Luther had adopted it from Occam to solve the problems that a fixed and limited receptacle implied, but it did give Luther the advantage of combining his stress upon the actual condescension of God in self-abasement to be one with us in our world, with a new dynamism in which he rejected the Greek and medieval idea of the reference of our thought to a point of absolute rest. However, the retention of the receptacle idea in Lutheran theology and its employment as an epistemological principle in the *finitum capax infiniti* prevented Lutheran theology from taking advantage of Luther's other insights, so that we find both the early and later *kenoticists* not only reproducing within the realm of Christology the same problems but also the same basic solutions to those problems found in the realist and nominalist approaches in the medieval world.

As we look back upon these questions it seems very evident that the essential intention of Roman, Lutheran, and Reformed accounts of the real presence of Christ was the same, and indeed that the pure theological content of their statements was pretty uniform, but what divided them so sharply was the alien concept of the receptacle and the dubious theological structures to which it gave rise in its advocates and also in its opponents. At this point Greek patristic theology was scientifically far in advance of Medievals and Protestants in its relational and differential concept of space. Now that modern science has shown us that the receptacle notion of space is untenable even for natural science, we ought to be more disposed to treat it as a non-theological intrusion into Christian doctrine and to work out in the modern context the kind of theological structure which the Early Church achieved in theirs. It is rather unfortunate that the old container-concept of space should have been reintroduced into the discussion between Lutheran and Reformed theologians in the valuable study, *Marburg Revisited*,[1] notably by Professor M. J. Heinecken. Let scientific thinking in theology cut away this idea altogether from our understanding of the real presence and there seems no theological ground for further division in this crucial issue.

We may now consider the conceptions of Order and Succession in the modern context. These notions suffered damage very early in the development of Western thought, in the assimilation to the doctrine of Order of the receptacle idea, as we have already noted, but also in considerable change that came over the Cyprianic conception of the principate of Peter in the College of Apostles through a pre-Christian notion of succession taken from Roman law but quite foreign to Biblical thought. The grafting of these different notions together can be traced in the legal formalizations of Leo the Great, but the concepts of Order and Succession that emerged became rigidly entrenched in Roman Catholic thought not only through the work of the canon lawyers but through the static structures and cataphatic conceptualism that grew up

---

[1] Edited by P. C. Empie and J. I. McCord, Augsburg Publishing House, Minneapolis, 1966.

within the Aristotelian and container notion of space. Similar problems have appeared in modern times with the rise and dominance of Newtonian science, when space came to be thought of as a container independent of what takes place in it and regarded as an inertial system exercising an absolute role in the whole causal structure of classical physics. Here the primary scientific questions were no longer as to the abstract essences or quiddities of things, but were concerned with concrete particularity. This yielded a view of matters of fact within isotropic space and time as discontinuous particles whose relationships were conceived in mechanistic terms. The objectivist structures that came out of this, found even in Protestant scholasticism, Lutheran and Reformed, were consistent with the static notion of space in the Newtonian world-view.

In this context the Roman notion of Succession in Orders became even more difficult since time as well as space formed the absolute receptacle or container within which all events were conceived as taking place. It was inevitable that the transmission of grace through space and time by means of ecclesiastical vessels and offices should be expounded in mechanistic concepts. This was impossible for Reformed theology which had tried to operate with a relational view of space and time on the patristic model, in which thought was developed in two directions, in accordance with the nature of the Creator who transcends all space and time and in accordance with the nature of the creature subject to space and time, but took its basic pattern from the interaction of divine and human agency in Jesus Christ. However, it was particularly difficult for Lutheran thought because it shared with Newtonian science a receptacle view of space and its latent dualisms. Here Luther's notion of the mathematical point in the relation between God and the world and Kant's 'Copernican' revolution in which space and time were regarded as *a priori* forms of intuition outside the range of experience, were brought together in the search for an answer to Roman dogma. But when the answer was worked out, it was at the expense of confining the acts of God to the transcendental side of a radical dualism between God and this world, and even Reformed theology as we find it in

Schleiermacher's *Glaubenslehre* joined Lutheran Protestantism in taking the same line. This proved unacceptable to the Anglicans, as well as to many Lutheran and Reformed Churchmen, who saw that it was no answer to the Roman conception of succession to reduce extension to a spaceless and timeless relation of Spirit. Moreover, the Neo-Protestant attitude to succession in space and time introduced a fatal chasm into the understanding of history, a Gnostic split between 'the Christ of faith' and 'the Jesus of history', and therefore the reduction of the historical Jesus to a vanishing-point. These are the ultimate questions at stake in the concern for historical succession in the ministry of the Gospel, and it is not surprising that many Lutheran and Reformed theologians, as well as Anglicans, have wanted to insist on an integral relation between historical Succession and Orders as an indispensable witness to the reality of the Gospel and its relevance to us in our historical existence in this world of space and time. What divides the Church here is not (or should not be) doctrine, but pseudo-theological structures (Roman and Protestant) that have arisen through the introduction of alien and irrelevant ideas into theology.

The curious thing is that the difficulties raised on one side by the receptacle view of space and time and on the other side by the reduction of space and time to *a priori* mental processes are still with us in the debates of the ecumenical movement, whereas this contraposition is both a confusion in theology and an anachronism in science. Pure theology will not allow us to resolve away spatial and temporal relations or escape from the rational structures that the creation of space and time import, nor will it allow us to elaborate notions of space and time *in abstracto* and then to use them as fixed forms within which to interpret the work of God, forcing our understanding of His grace into their rigid mould. Nor will modern science allow us to think in these ways, since four-dimensional geometry and relativity theory have destroyed the conceptions of space and time as absolute either in the form of receptacles independent of what goes on inside them or as conditioning abstractions existing only in the human consciousness. Instead they force us to think in terms of a space-time continuum which, far from being amorphous, is the dynamic bearer of rational structure, yet one that does not have the rigid causal character attributed to it in the mechanistic interpretation of classical physics. Here another scientific question is being asked, as to the field of connection in which things are found, which yields the view that they are not related like discrete particles in static, isomorphic space but are connected in a continuous flow of motion. Space and time thus become relational concepts bound up with the movement of contingent events of which they are functions, while succession is regarded as a sequence in space and time of continuous and coherent structures. All this does not mean that Christian theology must now give up the old scientific notions of space in order to adopt a more modern one, but that in dialogue with natural science in its struggle to understand space and time in the natural processes of this world, theology on its part must strive to develop a strictly *theological* understanding of space and time in the light of God's interaction with this world as revealed in the incarnation of His Son in space-time, and in that context develop an adequate theological account of Succession in relation to Order.

In bringing this discussion to a close, we may note that scientific thinking in the ecumenical context is engaged in a task not unlike that in which we find ourselves in modern natural science. As we have noted, in classical physics the primary question that was directed to nature concerned concrete particularity, which gave rise to a particulate view of nature which has reached its supreme point in the corpuscular theory of light. In more recent science there has developed the concept of the field from the question as to the connecting-links of events in the whole continuum of space and time, out of which has come the undulatory theory of light. The raising of this question and the development of the notion of the field of relations has modified the way in which the particulate aspect of nature was regarded; but while the first question had to be developed in observational language and mechanistic concepts, the second question which was concerned with what is real but not observable had to develop a symbolic language and relational concepts. But matters cannot be left there, so that we are engaged at the moment in developing unitary theories at a higher level in which the results of the different approaches may be co-ordinated in such a way as to allow us to penetrate more deeply into the immanent rationality of nature and allow the inner coherence of the created universe to shine through to us.

Ecumenical thinking is now forcing theology along a parallel path. After the basis had been laid for positive theology by the Church Fathers, Christian thought concentrated upon God's *Being-in-His-Act* and developed accordingly static-ontic structures of thought which reached a high point in medieval theology. With the Reformation, however, different questions were asked and Christian thought began to concentrate upon God's *Act-in-His-Being*, and developed dynamic-noetic structures of thought out of reflection upon the saving work of Christ. Here we have the transition from medieval to modern times which corresponds with the great shift in the concepts and language found in the various sciences. But this movement of thought was arrested somewhat in theology as in empirical science in the dominance of Newtonian thought with its dualism between space and matter, or volume and mass, and its principle of the inertial system. Thus in Protestantism we have a return to scholasticism with its static and objectivist modes of thought. However, this broke down in deistic dualism, so that when the more dynamic aspects of Reformation thought were released they were pursued in detachment from ontology in a way that would have made Luther's hair stand on end! Thus, near the middle of the nineteenth century there developed a more dynamic and dialectical approach which corresponded in its way with the scientific development after the Faraday–Maxwell concept of the field began to play a significant role. This movement in Protestant theology was to run out into the sand first in romantic idealism and then in the theology of timeless events. But now once again Protestant theology has become concerned with the interconnection between the dynamic and ontological that characterized the great Reformers. It does not look as though this will or can succeed if it is confined within the development of Reformation theology, for what is needed is advance to a higher level of thought in which a unitary theology comprises the two historic approaches to the *Being* of God as discerned in His Acts, and to the *Acts* of God as they are discerned issuing from His Being.

This is surely the function of Ecumenical Theology in which modern scientific thinking must be brought to bear upon the whole history of the Church and its understanding of the Gospel in all its major communions and traditions. But it will succeed in that only if it is prepared for immense scientific labour in laying bare the fundamental structure of all theology in its logical simplicity as well as its coherent connections, and in developing at the same time the cognitive instruments appropriate to the nature of God and His saving acts in space and time. So far Christian theology has not done this, for throughout its history it has relied on the kind of logic that has been developed in other areas of knowledge and tried to apply it to its own subject-matter, with damaging effect. If Christian theology is to undertake this task it must surely undergo a change similar to that which has been taking place in natural science after the discovery of the new geometries applicable to space and time. Before then geometry was pursued independently of empirical science as an axiomatic, deductive science on its own, but now it has become a natural science indissolubly bound up with physics—that is to say, geometrical structures are studied as they arise in and with the actual knowledge of physical events. We have had a similar problem with what is called 'natural theology' which in medieval times (in sharp contrast with Patristic thought) was abstracted on its own as an antecedent science or as a *praeambula fidei*, and as such supplied the general frame of reference in which 'revealed theology' was interpreted. The same thing happened within Protestantism with the rise of deism when a new natural theology was developed in the modern style and which also became the frame of reference within which positive theology was given its interpretation. But that must not be allowed to continue, for the rational structure of knowledge of God cannot be scientifically studied except on the ground of actual knowledge where 'natural' theology is *natural* to the material content of that knowledge and developed in accordance with the nature of God as He revealed Himself in His Word and Acts. In other words, positive theology must develop its own 'four-dimensional geometry', as it were, which one might call the meta-science of theology, but it must be one that is indissolubly fused with positive and actual knowledge. This would do a great deal to obviate the tendency to impose arbitrarily mental patterns of our own excogitation upon the proper subject-matter of theology and at the same time enable us to develop the inner coherence and unitary structure of the knowledge of God in and through Jesus Christ with all its compelling results in ecumenism.

IV WORD AND SPIRIT

6

The Word of God and the Response of Man[1]

By the Word of God is meant not man's word about God but quite definitely God's own Word as God Himself lives and speaks it—Word as personal mode and activity of God's Being. Yet we have to do with the Word of God only as it has been addressed to us and has actually reached us, Word that has called forth and found response in our hearing and understanding and living —otherwise we could not speak of it. We do not begin, then, with God alone or with man alone, nor even with God speaking on the one hand and man hearing on the other hand, but with God and man as they are posited together in a movement of creative self-communication by the Word of God. This is not Word in which God exists only in and for Himself or which He speaks to Himself alone, but Word by which He creates and upholds other realities around Him and gives them room for their relations with Him. It is the mode of His Being in which God goes forth to meet man, freely relating His divine Life to him within the conditions of his creaturely nature, and in which He sustains man in his meeting with God, enabling him freely to relate his human life to the majesty of the divine Nature. It is in this togetherness and openness between God and man that God's self-revelation to man takes place. A profound reciprocity is created in which God addresses His Word to man by giving it human form without any diminishment of its divine reality as God Himself speaks it, and in which He enables man to hear His Word and respond to

---

[1] Lecture given to the session of *Académie Internationale des Sciences Religieuses* at Liebfrauenberg, Goersdorf, France, on 11 October 1968, and to the Faculty of Theology, University of Louvain, on 14 October 1968.

it without any cancellation of his human mode of being. The nature of the reciprocity is such that in assuming human form the Word of God summons an answering movement from man toward God which is taken up into the movement of the Word as a constitutive part of God's revelation to man. Thus the Word of God communicated to man includes within itself meeting between man and God as well as meeting between God and man, for in assuming the form of human speech the Word of God spoken to man becomes at the same time word of man in answer to God.

It is of course in the revelation of God actualized in our historical human existence through the instrumentality of Israel and in Jesus Christ the Word made flesh, in whom that actualization of divine revelation was brought to its fulfilment in acutely personal form, that we learn this about the Word of God and the response of man. We do not derive it from an analysis of the concrete life-situations of ancient Israel or the objectified forms of proclamation and worship found in the primitive Church, but directly from the activity of the Word Himself who as the source of human being has penetrated through the barriers of its estrangement, opened it out to the light and understanding of God and established a two-way connexion between God and man in the incarnation where the human response is true and faithful to the divine revelation, and not in the last analysis just a refracted form of man's self-understanding. This is Jesus Christ, the Interpreter and Mediator between man and God, who, as God of God in unqualified deity and as Man of man in unqualified humanity, constitutes in the unity of His incarnate Person the divine–human Word, spoken to man from the highest and heard by him in the depths, and spoken to God out of the depths and heard by Him in the highest. He is not only the Word of God come to man and become man, but He who as man bears and is the Word of God, the Word not only as God utters it but the same Word as heard, uttered and lived by man, and who as such carries in Himself the vicarious actuality, and conveys in Himself the active possibility, of true and faithful response on the part of all men to God's Word. It is thus in the form of sheer humanity in all its lowliness, weakness

and darkness that God's Word has reached us and made provision for free and adequate response on our part, but in such a
way that far from being a dispensable medium to be discarded
as soon as the target is reached, the humanity of the Word, God's
condescension to be one with us in our humanity, remains the
proof that in His own eternal Being He is not closed to us, and
the manifestation of His freedom to unveil Himself to man and
share with him His own divine Life.

It is upon this humanity of the Word in Jesus that we must
reflect deeply if we are to penetrate into the inner relation between
the Word of God and man's response, but we must not forget
that He is word of man in answer to God only in that He is first
and foremost Word of God become man. What did it mean,
then, for the eternal Word of God, *as Word*, to take creaturely
and human form, and thus to be heard *as word* by man?

I

In Himself the Word of God is quite independent of what He
has made. As the creative source and ground of all finite being He
maintains it in a binding relation to Himself but He is not bound
to it through any necessary relation of being or operation such as
that between cause and effect. He produces it freely by calling it
into being out of nothing and gives it a reality of its own which
He preserves and respects, and He Himself remains sovereignly
free over against it. He does not impart His substance to it; His
Life is not implicated in it; He does not communicate to it His
divine nature—and therefore He is known and understood only
on the free ground of His own self-subsistent Being. But He does
give form and order to finite being, limiting, determining and
enlightening it and thereby makes it comprehensible. He confers
upon it a created rationality different from, yet dependent on,
His own transcendent rationality, and thus gives it an inner law
of its own which is not self-explanatory, to be sure, but which
endures before God as the truth and goodness of created being
upheld by His eternal Word. It is into this created rationality (or
logos) that the Word (or *Logos*) of God enters, assimilating it to
Himself in the incarnation, in order to become Word to man

through the medium of human word and in order to provide from the side of man for an appropriate response in truth and goodness toward God.

This created rationality takes two main forms, *number* and *word*, corresponding to impersonal and personal being. Different though they are they come together in man, in the interrelation and inseparability of his physical and spiritual existence in space and time, and they operate together in the emergence of the universe as it is explored and scientifically built up through man's inter-action with nature and as its inherent rationality is brought to co-ordinate expression in mathematical and verbal language. Number is the rationality of the creation in its form as determinate event, the rationality of immanence and necessity which is mute in itself but which may be brought to articulation through man in so far as he thinks it under the compulsion of the physical nature of things. Word is the rationality of the creation in which it reaches beyond its fixed and mute condition, the rationality of transcendence and freedom in which man as the crown and priest of creation has the function of shaping formal instruments through which he may bring being to disclose itself in accordance with its manifold nature. Both forms of rationality are needed, but it is in and through man alone that they emerge into the open, so that it is by man's grasp and handling of them that the creation, including man, attains to its full being. The development of scien-tific knowledge is not something alien to the creation, imposed upon it *ab extra*, but is part of its proper development and thus a manifestation of its inherent nature. Just as the creation is given to produce life in itself, so it is given to produce its own articula-tion and thus to rise above its mute and confined condition. Number cannot come to expression apart from word, that is, without the acquisition of language through which man can stand over against his environment, designating its features and presenting them to himself as objects for reflexion and computa-tion in order that he may organize and enlarge his knowledge of the world. On the other hand, word cannot fulfil this role apart from number, that is, without the realm of the determinate and immutable which in virtue of its inherent rationality supplies the fixed medium for the development of intelligible systems of representation and at the same time acts as the external control required for consistency and universality in communication. Thus number and word find articulation in two co-ordinated levels of rationality in which each requires the other but in which word is the formal means by which the creation is delivered from being trapped in itself and is made open to what is above and beyond it. In this context the inherent rationality of the physical creation is seen not to be self-contained but to call for a transcendent rationality for its explanation and meaning.

Now the Word of God did not enter this sphere of created rationality as a stranger, for in the incarnation He came to His own, but He did enter into what was creaturely and contingent and therefore utterly different: and this *difference* must be taken into account. In the Creator Himself, Word, Person and Act are one and undivided, but in the creature they fall apart. With us word is different from act. We speak, but have to exert additional power in order to fulfil what we say in deeds. We act, but our acts are not personal in themselves. Our speech and our action do not coincide in the unity and power of our person. Act and person, word and person, word and act are all separate—they are not unrelated, but their relationship is conditioned by physical existence and is refracted and strung out in time. With God it is not so. He encounters us as One whose Word and whose Act belong to the self-subsistence of His Person. What He speaks takes place of itself, for it is filled with the power of His Person, the power by which He is what He is and by which He lives His own personal Life in absolute self-sufficiency and freedom. His power to act is not other than the power of His Person or the power of His Word. He is in Person identical with His Word, and His Word is itself His Act. However, when the Word of God condescended to participate in created existence in order to become Word to man, personally addressing him in the medium of human speech and physical event in space and time, He entered into the divided and finite condition of word, person and act and into the duality of number and word, that characterize created reality. He came as genuine man, physically conditioned in space and time, in whom willing, speaking and doing are different, who thinks and forms judgements, whose acts follow upon his decisions, whose words are in addition to his person and whose works are in addition to his words, but who in none of these things is self-sufficient, for as man he lives and thinks and speaks and acts only in inseparable relation to his fellow-men and in dependence upon the physical creation. Clearly, for the eternal Word of God to become understandable and communicable in the mode and character of word to man He had to share to the full in the space–time distinctions and connexions of human existence in this world and operate within the finite conditions of created rationality. This is not to say, of course, that He ceased to be the Word He is in the Creator, but rather that He appropriated human form within the frame of earthly life and action and speech in such a way as to take up the frail and finite conditions of the creature into Himself not merely as the earthen vessel of the Word of God but as His actual speaking of it to us. In Jesus Christ the Word has become physical event in space and time, meets us in the indissoluble connexion of physical and spiritual existence, and is to be understood within the co-ordinate levels of created rationality. The unity in God between Person, Word and Act has been made to overlap and gather within its embrace the differences between person, word and act in the creature, so that they are allowed to mediate God's Word to man in time through a oneness between Christ's human utterance about God and God's self-utterance to man. Expressed otherwise, in the hypostatic union between God and man in Jesus Christ there is included a union between the Word of God and the word of man, but in such a way that far from being displaced in some Apollinarian fashion the word of man is fully and finally established in its genuine humanity through the regenerating and humanizing work of the Word made flesh.

There is another side to all this, however, which is supremely important. When the Word of God became man, He came to His own, but His own did not receive Him, for although they derived their being from Him they had rebelled against Him and had fallen into darkness and enmity. Thus it was not only into our contingent and finite condition that the Word of God had to penetrate, but into our sin and alienation where we are subject to the thraldom of evil power, into our guilty existence under the sentence of divine judgement, and into the disintegration of our human being in death. He came, therefore, to share our lost and enslaved existence where it was breaking up under the corrosion of sin and guilt, disease and want, death and judgement, and to enter into the disordered state of our created rationalities in which finite distinctions are damaged and distorted into contradictions, in order to engage with the inhuman forces of darkness that had encroached upon the bodies and minds of men, to struggle with the perverse nature of an alienated creation, to meet the full hostility of evil by accepting and bearing it in Himself, and to make an end of it in His own vicarious life and death. But throughout all He by whom all men were made and in whom they consist lived as man on earth and in history a life of holiness, trust and love in filial obedience to the heavenly Father, thus carrying the human nature He had received from us through darkness, conflict, rejection and judgement into new being in His resurrection from the dead. By being completely and unreservedly God's Word incarnate in the fulness of grace and truth He was able from within our estranged and impaired existence to deliver man from subjection to futility and negation, recreate his relation to God, realize perfect humanity on the earth, and to offer in and through Himself man's true response in person, word and act to God the Creator. God's Word has reached and found common understanding and reciprocity with us through the anguish and passion of incarnation and atonement and through the rebirth of man in the integrity and wholeness of his physical and spiritual existence in the resurrection. In the whole life, death and resurrection of Jesus God Himself was directly at work affirming as good what He had made and making good His own Word in the creation of the world.

That is what was involved in every act of mercy and healing in which the commanding fiat of the Creator was found on the lips of Jesus. As the Evangelists make clear in their reporting, the different miracles of Jesus were concerned with the saving of creation in its spiritual and physical conditions, but the way in which they took place, through His sharing in our earthly existence in all its distress and limitation, revealed that only through the full participation of the Creator with us in our creaturely and human life can atonement for sin and redemption from evil power issue in the actual restoration of what God has made. That is surely why the Fourth Gospel with all its immense stress upon the humanity and obedience of the Son opens with the Prologue in which we are told that the Creator Word has become flesh, Himself one of the creatures made through Him, in order to effect the enlightenment and regeneration of man by working within his creaturely existence and serving it from below and by sharing with him His own sanctified humanity. Without the incarnation of the Creator Word the fallen world would crumble away finally and irretrievably into nothingness, for then God would simply be letting go of what He had made and it would suffer from sheer privation of being. But the incarnation has taken place. Once and for all, the Creator Word has entered into the existence of what He has made and bound it up with His own eternal Being and Life embodied in Jesus Christ, yet without violating its creaturely nature. In this union of the Creator with the creature the eternal Word of God who is the ground of man's existence from beyond his existence has now become also the ground of his existence within his existence, undergirding and sustaining it from within its natural processes in such a way as to establish his reality and meaning as human being and to realize his distinctive response toward God in the fulness of his creaturely freedom and integrity.

Let it be stressed, however, that all this is achieved by the Word of God, not merely as in the original creation by direct fiat, but by condescending to participate in finite being, submitting to its limitations and operating within its struggles and structures, thus fulfilling God's saving purpose for the creation in and through the inner determination of His incarnate life as Man on earth and in history. Such was the life and mission of Jesus Christ the Word made flesh who mediated between God and man, reconciling them in and through Himself, and so established a correlation and correspondence between God's self-giving and man's receiving within which alone God's revelation could be actualized in man and a true and faithful response could be yielded by man to God.

Here we arrive again at the point we noted at the outset, that in effecting His self-communication to man the Word of God assimilates the hearing of man to itself as a constitutive part of God's revelation, but now two things must be emphasized; Jesus Christ is Himself the hearing man included in the Word of God, and He is that in a final and definitive way. In the Gospels we do not have to do simply with the Word of God and the response of man, but with the all-significant middle term, the divinely provided response in the vicarious humanity of Jesus Christ. As the humanity of the Word through whom we have our being the humanity of Christ occupies a unique place in the creative ground of our humanity, and as the humanity in which atonement and reconciliation have been perfected it fulfils a representative and substitutionary role in all our relations with God, including every aspect of human response to Him: such as trusting and obeying, understanding and knowing, loving and worshipping. Jesus Christ is presented to us in the Gospels as He who in and through His humanity took our place, acting in our name and on our behalf before God, freely offering in Himself what we could not offer and offering it in our stead, the perfect response of man to God in a holy life of faith and prayer and praise, the self-offering of the Beloved Son with whom the Father is well pleased. And so to those who receive Him and believe in Him, power and freedom are given to become sons of God: not in virtue of any natural birth through the will of the flesh or the will of man, but in virtue of their birth from God, a rebirth from above. Now that God's saving grace has taken this way, in the provision of man's true and faithful response in the vicarious humanity of Jesus Christ, it thereby invalidates all other ways of response. Here there operates, so to speak, a theological form of Fermat's principle in accordance with which the selection of one among other possible paths in the formulation of natural law sets the others aside as unentertainable and actually impossible. In Himself God is transcendently free and able to create other possibilities

—such as raising up children for Abraham from the stones of the Jordan—but the actual coming of His eternal Word into our contingent existence in Jesus Christ excludes every other way to the Father, and stamps the vicarious humanity of Christ to be the sole norm and law as well as the sole ground of acceptable human response to God. Hence the response to which man is summoned by the proclamation of the Word of God is not some arbitrary self-determination or independent self-expression on his part, but one derived from, grounded in, and shaped by the very humanity of the Word which originally gave him being as man and continues to sustain him in his human nature and spontaneity before God as well as in his engagement in the world of things and persons to which he belongs.

II

Hitherto we have been considering the fact that in order to be Word to man the Word of God became flesh, but now we must consider the fact that the Word came to *dwell* among us. That is to say, we have considered the relation of the Word of God to the response of man in terms of the humanity which the Word assumed in addressing him, and must now go on to consider the fact that in order to be heard and understood as Word it had to enter the speaker-hearer relationship within humanity and become speech to man, spoken and heard through the medium of human language. But language is rooted in a society and is kept alive by the exchange and development of thought that takes place through it. It is the currency of social being. Neither in God nor in man is word found in isolation but only in community. In God the Word subsists in the inner consubstantial relations of the Holy Trinity, and in man words have their existence in the public language of expression and communication developed by a community of persons bound together not only by a common world but by a common way of life and culture. Hence, if the Word of God is to enter the forum as speech to man through the medium of human words it must be directed to man in community, and if that Word creates reciprocity between God and man it must create a community of such reciprocity within human society as the appropriate medium of its continuing communication to man.

That is what happened between God and Israel, for the Word of God spoken to man did not operate in a vacuum but penetrated human existence in the particular life and history of one people elected as the instrument for the actualization of God's revelation in humanity and separated as a holy nation in whose midst God dwelt in an intimate way through the presence of His Word. The covenant relationship between God and Israel which this set up was a particularization of the one covenant of grace which embraced the whole of creation and constituted its inner bond and ground, and therefore carried in it the promise of a final universalization of God's revelation in which His Word would bring light and salvation to all the peoples of mankind and indeed a new heaven and a new earth.

Thus Israel became aware of itself as a people seized by the Word of God, constituted into a worshipping community open toward God, and charged with messianic destiny. The same mighty Word that created the world and ultimately lay behind every event in nature and in history was at work in its midst creating corporate reciprocity and using the responses it provoked, whether of assent or dissent, obedience or disobedience, blindness or enlightenment, apostasy or reform, as instruments for its deeper penetration into Israel's existence and the means through which it became understandable and communicable to man. As the Word of God invaded the social matrix of Israel's life, culture, religion and history, and clothed itself with Israel's language, it had to struggle with the communal meaning already embedded in it in order to assimilate it to God's revelation of Himself. For new understanding to take root within Israel, it had to take shape within Israel's language, and therefore it had to remould the inner structure of the society within which that language had its home and had to determine the whole history of Israel in its physical existence. Hence through the impact of the Word there were initiated in the tradition of Israel priestly and prophetic movements which entailed critical revision of previous ways of life, worship, and thought in order to break through the barriers of naturalistic and pagan convention that obstructed knowledge of the living God. New forms of worship, thought, and expression had to be created as the context within which the Word of God could be heard and understanding of it could be established, but in order that this orientation toward God could be habituated in its mind and existence Israel had to be subjected to ordeal by history through a long struggle of the Word with the perverse nature of man as it was forced into the open in Israel's intimate experience of divine judgement and mercy. And so throughout Israel's tradition the Word of God kept pressing for articulation within the corporate medium of covenant reciprocity and progressively took verbal and even written form through the shared understanding and shared response that developed in this people. The historical dialogue between God and Israel, in covenant and controversy, was maintained by a concentration of the speaker–hearer relation in a prophetic nucleus within Israelite society through which the Word of God assumed decisive form in the mouth of men and impinged relentlessly upon Israel's life, interpreting its history, determining its direction, calling it out to be people or church of God, and opening its future toward the incarnation. Thus Israel became in a unique way the bearer of God's Word to mankind and His corporate prophet among the nations of history.

That Word was encountered in historic Israel as yet only in its 'formable' state (to borrow an old Augustinian expression), for it was still in process of taking shape in the habits of the human mind and speech. But throughout its historical reciprocity with Israel the Word of God kept creating formal and empirical correlates of its own self-utterance through which it extended its activity and speech in space and time. Although they were by no means exhaustive transcripts of that self-utterance they came to be deposited in the Old Testament Scriptures, for in and through them men continued to hear God addressing them directly and backing up His Word by the living power and majesty of His divine Person. In this dynamic mode the Word of God pressed on through the life and experience of Israel toward final and definitive form, but for that reason the scriptural forms inspired by the

Spirit proclaimed far more than they could specify at the time and so by their very nature they pointed ahead to the full disclosure of the divine reality they served.

The whole fact of Israel entrusted with the oracles of God was itself a mighty response evoked by the Word of God out of the midst of history, but within Israel the Word of God was mediated in such a way that a divinely prepared form of obedient response was included within it. That is what we find in the prophetic message about the servant of the Lord through whose passion a new covenant would be inaugurated bringing redemption to Israel and a light to lighten the Gentiles, and that is what we find fulfilled at last in the birth of Jesus. God had adapted Israel to His purpose in such a way as to form within it a womb for the incarnation of the Word and a matrix of appropriate forms of human thought and speech for the reception of the incarnational revelation. And so Jesus was born of Mary, out of the organic correlation of Word and response in the existence of Israel, to be the Word of God made flesh in the life and language of man and to be that Word heard and expressed in the truth and grace of perfect human response to God. In Him God's Word has become speech to man through the medium of human words and speaks to men as man to man, for in Him God has graciously assumed our human speech into union with His own, effecting it as the human expression of the divine Word, and giving it as such an essential place in His revelation to man.

With the incarnation, however, we have moved into a decisively different situation from that which obtained in Old Testament times, for here the forms of thought and speech developed in ancient Israel are not only fulfilled but transcended and relativized by the final and permanent forms which the Word has taken in the life and teaching of Jesus Christ. That is the real ground for what Schleiermacher called 'the language-moulding power of Christianity'. It is not just a correlation between the Word of God and the transient response which it evokes, as the instrument of deeper and deeper penetration into human existence, which we have here. Rather is it such a profound integration between Word of God and word of man that they can no longer be separated out from each other. The humanity of the Word, even in His distinctive individuality and physical particularity, is not something that can be discarded like outworn clothing that has served its purpose in the past, for it is constituted the actual address of God's Word to man and is indissolubly bound up with its material content. Hence the basic forms of human thought and speech in which the incarnational revelation is mediated to us cannot be made the object of independent investigation in themselves as if they could be abstracted from their historical context and factual reference, nor can they be understood primarily from their place in the social and religious matrix of Israel or Church as if they could be interpreted merely out of the subjective states of those who received God's revelation, but from their place in the normative and definitive structure of the Word made flesh in His solidarity with human and physical being in space and time.

At this point, we must remember that human language has its place in the interaction of man's physical and spiritual existence and functions through the co-ordinate levels of created rationality corresponding to determinate event and personal behaviour. The introduction of any dichotomy into that situation would take away the ground of signification and open up a chasm of meaninglessness. Far from doing anything like that, the incarnation of the Word overcame the inner disruption in man's existence that had resulted from his estrangement from God and established again the unity and wholeness of his being in space and time. Hence in Jesus Himself, word and deed, language and event, were inextricably interwoven in His revealing activity. His words were done as well as spoken and His deeds spoke as much as His words, for in Him God's Word had become physical, historical event, while the very fact and existence of Jesus was itself Word of God. This conjunction between language and event in the interaction of the Word of God with nature is very evident in the parabolic teaching of Jesus. The parable was chosen, not to provide detachable symbolic forms through which human thought could be lifted up away from this world into some transcendental realm of Word, but as the means of setting man's hearing of the Word squarely within this-worldly reality, for it is there in the concrete situations of our earthly existence that God Himself meets us and addresses us. Thus the parable operates through co-ordinating the conceptual and symbolic levels of language, in much the same way as we saw word and number to be co-ordinated in the development and articulation of our scientific knowledge of nature. As such it both reveals the applicability of the Word to our earthly existence and shows the significant place given to this world in the incarnation of the Word of God. The parables, however, direct us above all to Jesus Christ Himself as the mystery of the Kingdom of God in our midst, for it is in Him that the reality of God meets us within the reality of this world. He is the one place on earth and in history where we may have such reciprocity with God that we may hear His Word and see His Face. Thus in their conjunction of language and event the parables of Jesus correspond to and reveal His nature as Word of God manifest in the flesh. The real text of the New Testament Scriptures is the humanity of Christ. He is God's exclusive language to us and He alone must be our language to God.

We must now consider more fully the transition that took place in the historical existence of Jesus Christ from His being Word of God to man to His being also word of man to man, communicable within the medium of man's exchange in thought and word with his fellow man. In Jesus Christ, as we have seen, we are presented with God's Word to man and man's obedient response to God incorporated into God's Word as an essential part of it. As such, Jesus Christ is God's self-address to man, but this self-address in order to achieve its end had to penetrate, take form and domicile itself within the address of man to man, as the Word of Christ abiding among men. The reciprocity established between God and man in Jesus Christ had to create room for itself within the reciprocities of human society, and the Word of God which had come 'plumb down from above' had to deploy itself in the horizontal dimensions of human existence in order to continue its speaking and acting throughout history. This involved the formation of a nucleus within the speaker-hearer relations of men, corresponding to and grounded in the communion between God and man embodied in Jesus Christ, as the controlling basis among believers for the extended communication of the Word of God, and the translation of the self-witness of Christ into witness to Christ, answering the normative pattern of His obedient humanity, as the specific form for the proclamation of God's Word to all men.

That is what took place in the apostolic foundation of the Church and in the apostolic formulation of the *kerygma*, both as parts of one movement in which Christ's self-address to man evoked and inspired a response in word and deed which He assimilated into union with His own response to God and effected as the authoritative expression of His own *kerygma* in the world. Thus, in the apostles as the receiving end of His revealing and reconciling activity, Jesus Christ laid the foundation of the Church which He incorporated into Himself as His own Body, and permitted the Word which He put into their mouth to take the form of proclamation answering to and extending His own in such a way that it became the controlled unfolding of His own revelation within the mind and language of the apostolic foundation. The apostolic proclamation of Christ was so geared into His self-proclamation that it was used by Him as the shared and corporate medium of understanding and communication through which He brought His Word in human and historical form to bear upon mankind throughout the ages. Just as the response of man in Christ was made a constituent element in the Word of God to man, so the response of the apostles was assumed by Christ into oneness with His own to form the means by which the Word of Christ reached out into history. Thus, through the apostolic witness and proclamation, it was Christ Himself who was at work testifying to the mighty acts whereby He had redeemed the world and offering Himself to men as their Saviour and Lord.

This then is the New Testament proclamation of the Word of God which already includes within itself the kind of responses to which it summons mankind. The response of the apostles which had been taken up into the proclamation was of a second-order nature compared to that of Christ, for the primary text of the Word remained that of the humanity of Christ Himself. Hence the proclamation of the Gospel announces to us that the true and faithful response of man to God has already been made in the self-offering of Christ on our behalf, and holds it out to us as the divinely appointed and provided response in which we may share freely as through the Spirit we participate in the vicarious obedience of the Word made flesh. The place given to the response of the apostles in the *kerygma* is certainly of authoritative and critical significance for the whole history of the Church, but its purpose there is to enable us to stand with the original witnesses under the impact of the Word they received and to be drawn into the sphere of its effective operation where we, like them, may learn to repent and believe the Gospel, give thanks to God and live in communion with Him. Thus, far from obtruding themselves or their own spirituality upon us, the apostles serve the *kerygma* by directing us back to the representative and vicarious humanity of Christ as the creative ground and normative pattern for the actualization of every response to God on our part.

III

We must now give some attention to specific forms of response that are called forth by the proclamation of the Word of God and show their relation to the response of Christ.

(a) *Faith*

Faith is undoubtedly a primary form of response to the Word of God, involving the elements of trust, assent and belief; but since in the biblical context God Himself in His own Person stands behind His Word and pledges Himself to us in it, faith is also understood as the faithfulness of man answering to and dependent upon the faithfulness of God as its ultimate ground. God does not break His Word, for in His Word God remains true both to Himself and to those to whom He sends His Word. His Word always fulfils its intention, actualizing itself in deeds and events that correspond faithfully to it, thus manifesting itself as God's Truth. The same applies, *mutatis mutandis*, to the human sphere, in which truth is found wherever word and event coincide, and a man is reckoned true and faithful when his deed is as good as his word. Thus God is said to keep truth or faith with His people and they are required to keep truth or faith with Him. In this the biblical understanding, faith subsists in the mutual relation of faithfulness between God and man involving consistency between word and event.

In these terms the incarnation is to be understood as the mighty act of God in which His Word has become event in our flesh in such a way that the event corresponds perfectly with His Word. Jesus Christ is the Truth of God actualized in our midst, the incarnate faithfulness of God, but He is also man keeping faith and truth with God in a perfect correspondence between His life and activity in the flesh and the Word of God. In Him there is utter consistency between God the Word revealing Himself to man and man hearing, believing, obeying, and speaking His Word. Not only is He the incarnation of the divine faithfulness but the embodiment and actualization of man's faithfulness in answer to God's; but as such He offers to God, and is toward God in His own person and life, our human response of faith and obedience to God. If it was in His humanity in entire solidarity with us that Jesus Christ stood in our place, and gave to God an account for us in His life and death, in utter faithfulness to God and to man, then this includes the fact that He believed for us, offering to God in His vicarious faithfulness, the perfect response of human faith which we could not offer.

That is what the Word of God proclaims to us in the Gospel, and therefore it summons us to respond by faith only as it holds out to us free participation in the faithful response of Christ already made on our behalf. Hence our response of faith is made within the ring of faithfulness which Christ has already thrown around us, when in faith we rely not on our own believing but wholly on His vicarious response of faithfulness toward God. In this way Christ's faithfulness undergirds our feeble and faltering faith and enfolds it in His own; but since His faithfulness enshrines within itself the faithfulness of God and the faithfulness of the Man Jesus, we are unable to disentangle our acts of faith in Christ from their implication in the eternal faithfulness of God.

Within this relation between the faithfulness of God and the faithfulness of man polarized through the incarnation of God's

Word there is another primary aspect of faith that must be taken into account, that in which it answers to the Word as *Event* and credits Word and Event in their correspondence with one another as the Truth of God in action. This is the aspect of faith in which the intellectual elements are prominent. It takes place within the created rationalities of space and time into which the Word made flesh assimilated Himself, and therefore exhibits itself in ways that reflect those forms of rationality in respect of necessity and freedom, immanence and transcendence. Here on the one hand, where we are up against the concrete actualities in nature and history through which God meets us, faith is the *assent* which we are forced to yield when we react to the given facts in accordance with their immanent nature and intelligibility. This involves an act of rational judgement, but one demanded and controlled by the firm structure of the objective reality, the physical and historical event in which we hear God's Word. On the other hand, when we are engaged in personal encounter with God in which His Word penetrates into our existence, creates reciprocity with us, and invites our response, faith is the willing *consent* which we yield to the Word in recognition of His transcendent majesty and intelligibility. This involves an act of rational understanding in which our minds are opened to grasp what is beyond their natural power, but which they freely acknowledge on the ground of its divine nature and self-evidence, the Grace and Truth of God in Jesus Christ.

Of course, faith does not comprise two different acts but one movement of response in which there are elements of freedom and compulsion corresponding to the mutual involution of Word and Event in God's self-revelation in Jesus Christ. He is proclaimed to us in the Gospel as at once objective historical Fact and personal Word of God and thus encounters us in the *kerygma* with a determinate rationality in His Being, and an articulate rationality in His Word through which He is disclosed to us in His Being. As Word of God come in the flesh who cannot be other than He is, Jesus Christ is known only in accordance with the innermost necessity of His Being, but far from overwhelming us with the immediacy of His divine nature He graciously meets us in the midst of our worldly distinctions and relations through the medium of His human nature and word, giving us freedom to listen to Him and understand Him, respond to Him and follow Him. Nevertheless, even when we know Him freely through the Truth of His Word our minds fall under the compulsion of the Truth of His Being. This is what the New Testament calls the obedience of faith' which is the willing assent of our mind to 'the claims of His divine Reality and the responsible commitment of our will to the saving efficacy of His activity in the flesh. Since there can be no faith apart from the acknowledgment of the historical actuality and reality of Jesus Christ and of the divine authority of His self-revelation in our worldly existence, the humanity of the incarnate Word remains the firm basis and law of our response; but since He encounters us in the personal medium of word and requires of us a response in the same medium, faith does not come to fruition unless the inner assent spontaneously translates itself into articulate acknowledgment and thanksgiving, that is, in Pauline language, unless confession with the mouth accompanies belief in the heart.

(b) *Worship*

From the point we have just reached it should be evident that worship is the natural expression of faith; but, let it be added, expression of faith in its objective orientation in the humanity of Christ, rather than subjective self-expression on the part of believers. Like faith, worship comprises elements of freedom and necessity bound up with language which is its natural medium and the nature of that to which it offers response.

We recall that language is the system of verbal signs which we develop in order to grasp things and present them to ourselves in such a way that we can stand over against them and think about them, and allow them to disclose themselves to us in forms appropriate to them. This applies in different ways to the world of things and the world of persons, but in both we are engaged in the rationality of acting in accordance of what is not-ourselves and enlarging our knowledge of it. In the world of persons, however, it is particularly with inter-personal transcendence that we are concerned, in which we distinguish ourselves from each other and communicate with each other. This is also the role which language plays in our worship of God. Worship is essentially a dialogical activity in which we stand over against God even when we draw near to Him, distinguishing His transcendent nature from ourselves, while relating ourselves appropriately to His holiness and majesty and responding thankfully to the mercy He extends towards us. By meeting us and entering into dialogue with us through His Word the transcendent God creates space for our 'transcendence' over against Him and at the same time creates between us and Himself the rational continuity in which reciprocity and communion can take place. And since God's Word comes to us in and through the medium of human language, it establishes our communion with God in the creaturely freedom that obtains between human speaking and responding, and summons us to formulate our human responses to Him within that freedom.

If language is to serve its purpose adequately in any field, it must be rightly related to the realities which it is used to signify, but as soon as that relation is damaged the disclosure of reality through it becomes distorted and the language itself becomes obscure. That is our perpetual difficulty in worship. Since our language is rooted in human society, it is psychologically and socially conditioned by naturalistic patterns of thought and speech that have already developed in it and are not appropriate to God, so that if they are used in the formulation of our responses to His Word they inevitably make things opaque. That is why worship calls for a great deal of refined activity on our part in purifying and adapting our liturgical language until it becomes, as far as possible in our pilgrim state, a transparent medium for communion with God in which we do not obstruct self-discourse on His part and are made open for heuristic vision on our part.

Since liturgical activity of this kind requires to be controlled and shaped by the reality it serves, we are inevitably thrown back upon the objective self-disclosure of God in Jesus Christ, for He is the one place in our humanity where the divine Light shines through to us undimmed and unobstructed by damaged relations or distorting forms of thought and speech; but in Jesus Christ we are given more than the creative mould for our human responses, we are provided with the very essence and core of man's worship of God. In His life, death, resurrection and ascension He offered Himself through the eternal Spirit in our name and on our behalf, presenting us in Himself to the Father, once and for all, so that He remains for ever our sole offering in deed and word with which we appear before God. We do not draw near to God in worship either with our own self-expression or empty handed, but with hands of faith filled with the self-oblation of Christ, for He constitutes in His vicarious humanity the eloquent reality of our worship.

In His covenant with Israel God not only promised to be their God and required of them to walk before Him and be perfect, but gratuitously provided for Israel in the sacred cult the appointed way of response in fulfilment of His divine requirement. The prophets, some of whom came from the priesthood, insisted that this vicarious response had to be enacted by way of obedience into the life and existence of Israel in order to be efficacious reality, and pointed ahead to the Servant of the Lord as the chosen instrument for its actualization. That is precisely what took place in Jesus Christ in the whole course of His obedience from His birth to His death on the Cross, for He fulfilled in Himself the Word of God tabernacling among men, the covenanted way of response to God set forth in the ancient cult, and constituted Himself our Temple, our Priest, our Offering and our Worship. It is therefore in His name only that we worship God, not in our own name, nor in our own significance but solely in the significance of Christ's eternal self-oblation to the Father.

(c) *The Holy Sacraments*

Both Baptism and Eucharist are acts of human response to the proclamation of God's Word, but they are above all the divinely appointed and provided ways of response and worship. They are not sacraments of what we do but Sacraments of the vicarious obedience of Christ once and for all offered in His finished work, and for ever prevalent before the Face of the Father in the heavenly intercession and mediation of His Son. We do not baptize ourselves but are baptized out of ourselves into Christ who loved us and gave Himself for us, and are incorporated into Him as members of His Body. Therefore we do not come before God in the Eucharist on the ground of what we have done even by way of response to His Word, for we come with nothing in our hands but the bread and wine, to feed upon Christ's Body and Blood and find shelter in His sacrifice and oblation on our behalf. In both these Sacraments of the Gospel the emphasis is undoubtedly on the human response vicariously fulfilled for us in Christ, and hence even the form (or the matter) of the Sacrament in each case is determined for us by dominical appointment. So far as the proclamation of the Gospel is concerned the Sacraments tell us that even when we respond to its call for repentance and faith, it is nevertheless not on our repentance and faith that we must rely but solely on that which Christ has already done and continues to do, freely made available for us in and through the Sacraments. As such, the Sacraments provide the natural basis within our daily physical existence for free and spontaneous response to the Word of God in which we do not have to keep looking over our shoulders to see whether our response is good enough. The very fact that in our response we are called to rely entirely upon the steadfast and incorruptible response of Christ made on our behalf frees us from the anxieties begotten of ulterior motivation and evokes genuine freedom and joy in our responding to God. So far as the worship of the Church is concerned the Sacraments tell us that liturgical language and activity derive their true form through assimilation to the vicarious life and work of Jesus Christ and that they may truly exhibit in themselves conformity to the normative pattern of worship in the humanity of Christ in so far as they make room for Him and direct us to Him as the actualized essence and core of man's true worship of God. That is why it is finally the Eucharistic celebration in union with the proclamation of the Word that gives shape to the Christian liturgy and mission.

Sacramental response has its place within the all-embracing response of faith to the proclamation of the Word of God and shares with it an inner relation to the Word through their joint inclusion within the covenanted faithfulness of God incarnated in

Christ. Although He is equally active in Word and in Sacrament, a significant distinction must be noted. The conjunction of the Sacraments with proclamation means that Christ will not allow the Word proclaimed to return to Him void but insists on actualizing in us the promises of redemption and regeneration that are extended to us in it. Thus the Sacraments themselves proclaim that as the Word made flesh Jesus Christ is effectively at work among us not only in the unity of His divine and human natures but in the unity of His spiritual and physical human being, healing and reintegrating man's broken and divided existence. Thus whereas faith corresponds more to the activity of the Word as Word, sacramental participation corresponds more to the activity of the Word as Event, for by their nature the Sacraments have to do with our physical as well as our spiritual being: we are baptized in body as well as in soul, and it is into our bodies that we take the bread and wine, feeding upon the Body and Blood of Christ and not just upon His Word and Spirit.

Behind this lies the profound integration between redemption and creation which we have already discussed in the incarnate life and work of Christ. He came not only to make expiation for our guilt and to forgive our sins, but by overcoming the destructive powers of evil to remove the threat to our existence and to re-create our being as the human children of the heavenly Father. Although He entered into our fragmented and disintegrating existence and took His human nature from us, in His holy Humanity the rift between spiritual and physical existence which characterizes our fallen human nature has been healed. Thus He is not less real in terms of our this-worldly reality nor less historical in terms of our historical existence, but rather all the more fully real and all the more truly historical because He has vanquished in Himself the forces that corrode and demolish our worldly and human existence in space and time. That is the Christ who gives Himself to us in Word and Sacrament and grants us through the power of His Spirit to participate in Him, He who has already bound up our existence with Himself and who as the incarnate, crucified and risen Lord present within it, ever sustains it in its reconciled relation to God.

In this perspective the specific function of the Sacraments is seen to be directed to the tension between the physical and the spiritual that continues to characterize a world waiting for the redemption of the body and to the tension between the state of the world already redeemed by Christ and its state in the future consummation when He will return to make all things new. They erect in the midst of history the covenanted relation appointed by Christ which embraces those tensions within an indissoluble and enduring bond in Him, so that far from allowing them to become radical breaks which would plunge us into chaos and futility they make them to serve the redemptive and recreative purpose of God, just as in the Cross God made the terrible sin of men in the death of Jesus to minister to our healing and forgiveness. Thus like the miracles of Jesus the Sacraments are prophetic signs that have to do with the saving of creation. As the Sacraments of God's inter-action with our physical existence in Jesus Christ they are the counterparts in our ongoing life to the deeds of grace and power in the historical life of Jesus in which He allied Himself with man against the forces of evil that had overtaken him, reclaiming lost humanity, not by accusing men in their sickness and sin but by shouldering the burden of their sickness and sin upon Himself, not by throwing the responsibility back upon them but by taking the responsibility upon Himself. As such, the Sacraments both call for and provide a response in which the interaction of the spiritual and the physical is exhibited here and now in anticipation of the new creation. They will not allow us therefore to respond to the proclamation of the Word of God only in some intellectual or merely spiritual way, for in and through them the movement of faith reaches its fruition as lived and acted response to the coming of the Word of God into our space and time, in thankful acknowledgment of the fact that all our responses, physical and spiritual, are upheld by Christ from within our existence and are enfolded in His one all-embracing response to the Father on our behalf.

(d) *Christian Service*

Christian service is the form of our response in which we are not partially but completely committed in the whole of our being before God, and which we discharge not occasionally but in the whole of our life and work. It is the form of service yielded out of an existence that has come under the compelling and commanding reality of what has taken place in Jesus Christ on our behalf. It is not to be thought of, therefore, as the spontaneous expression of love arising out of an autonomous existence of the Christian, intrinsically intelligible in its own operation and enshrining its own freely chosen motivation, but as *service*, the ministry of love heteronomously grounded in the incarnation of the Word and taking its essential form from the pure self-giving of God in the servant-existence and mission of Jesus. It is service in obedience to His commandment of love, yet it is spontaneous and free response because it is emancipated from the necessity of having to supply its own intelligible ground and is cut free from all anxiety and ulterior motivation by being grounded in the vicarious service of Christ in His selfless fulfilment of the love of God for all men. But incorporating Himself among us in the form of a servant He has incorporated our servant-existence in Himself, and thereby He has given it structure and shape, both through the obedience which He rendered in our nature unconditionally to the Father and through the love which in our nature He poured out in unrestrained compassion for all men. Thus Jesus Christ constitutes in Himself, in His own vicarious human life and service, the creative source and norm and pattern of all true Christian service. It is only in and through this Jesus Christ that Christian service can be fulfilled in which loving service looks for no reward beyond the knowledge that it falls under the commanding reality of Jesus Christ and looks for no thanks from those to whom service is rendered because it is done out of thankfulness to Him.

We recall that in Jesus Christ the Word of God has established reciprocity with us in the conditions, structures and limitations of our creaturely existence and within the alienation, disorder and disintegration of our human being where we are subject to the wasting power of evil and the divine judgement upon it, in order to lay hold of our world and sustain it from below, to recreate its relation to the Creator and realize its true response to Him as God and Father of all. That is to say, in Jesus Christ the transcendent Rationality of God has planted itself within the created order where its bounds, structures and connections break down under the negation of evil, in order to reintegrate spiritual and physical existence by setting up its own law within it, and restore it to wholeness and integrity in the form, as it were, of a meeting of the Rationality of God with itself in the midst of estranged existence and in the depths of its disorder. In this way, the incarnation has affected the whole creation, confirming the primordial act of the Word in conferring order and rationality upon it.

That is the world in which Christian service is now fulfilled, the world of men whose very existence is sustained in its relation to God by the hidden presence of the incarnate, crucified and risen Christ within it, overcoming the negation and irrationality of evil, and the world of nature whose reality is maintained in its relation to God by the immanent presence of the Creator Word who will not suffer it to fall away into meaninglessness and futility. It is the world in which, through Jesus Christ the Word made flesh, man is reconciled to existence and nature is not alien to man, for all things, visible and invisible, are reconciled and gathered up in Him as their Head and Lord. Just as Jesus Christ, made of woman, made under the law, fulfilled His servant-existence within the created rationalities of this world, for our sake, so the disciples of Jesus Christ are sent by Him to fulfil their servant-existence, in the law to Christ, within the created rationalities of the world He has redeemed, for His sake—i.e. within the world of word and number, or of persons and things. We cannot divorce the one from the other, for even in ourselves spiritual and physical existence have been reconciled, so that it is in the wholeness of our new being in Christ that we must look out on the world of personal and impersonal nature. We cannot hold apart the ministry of love from the activity of science, nor may we pursue our scientific exploration of the universe except in obedience to the God of love. In both forms of created rationality we must fulfil our service as those who in and through Jesus Christ are connected up with the transcendent Rationality of God, but as those whose service is assimilated to the pattern which Christ instituted in Himself when He fulfilled His own ministry in the humility, selflessness and weakness of pure service, and entirely renounced the use of any kind of power which might betray the nature of that ministry as service.

If we are to follow this Jesus in the modern world we must surely learn how to apply scientific knowledge and method to such terrible problems as hunger, poverty, and want, without falling into the temptation to build up power-structures of our own, through ecclesiastical prestige, social success or political instrumentality, in order to make our ministry of compassion effective within the power-structures of the world, for then we would contract out of Christian service as *service* and betray the weakness of Jesus. On the other hand, if we are to engage in scientific exploration of the universe, in response to the Word of God incarnate in Jesus Christ by whom it was made, we must learn to respect the nature of all created things, using pure science to bring their mute rationality into such articulation that the praises of the Creator may resound throughout the whole universe, without falling into the temptation to exploit nature through an instrumentalist science in the interest of our own self-aggrandizement and lust for power, for then also we would contract out of Christian service as *service* and sin against the hiddenness of Jesus in the world. No doubt, the created rationalities of word and number are very different, as different as the world of persons and the world of things, but they both go back to the same source in the transcendent Rationality of God and they are both brought together in the incarnation of God's Word in Jesus Christ, for they are upheld and sustained by Him. Therefore our service in the realm of word and our service in the realm of number must be co-ordinated through Jesus Christ in our common response to the love of God.

7

The Epistemological Relevance
of the Holy Spirit[1]

I

In no authentic knowledge do we begin with epistemology and then on the ground of theory independently argued go on to develop our actual knowledge. Far less can we pose in abstraction the question, 'How can we know God?' and then in the light of the answers we reach go on to examine and explicate what we know. Only on the ground of our actual knowledge of God may we develop an epistemology of it, for the form cannot be separated from the content or the method from the subject-matter of that knowledge. It is God who makes possible our knowledge of Him by giving Himself to us as the object of our knowing and by bringing us into a relationship with Him in which we are made capable of knowing Him, but within that relationship it is the nature of God as the given object of our knowledge that prescribes for us the mode of knowing Him. Thus while knowledge of God is grounded in His own being and activity, it takes shape within our human being and activity as human knowledge of God.

But is it meaningful to speak of the epistemology of the Spirit? Certainly we do not have any knowledge of God apart from the Spirit, for God is Spirit and we know Him in truth as we know Him in the Spirit. Nor can we have an independent epistemology of the Spirit as if He had His own epistemological ground apart from the Father and the Son, but are we not concerned in the

[1] Originally published in honour of G. C. Berkouwer in *Ex Auditu Verbi* (J. H. Kok, Kampen, 1965), pp. 272–96.

specific activity of the Spirit with that aspect of our knowing of God where epistemological forms break off and where we are up against acts of God that are not only inexplicable from the side of man but quite ineffable? Thus while the Holy Spirit is at work in our knowledge of God, in the nature of the case there can be no epistemology of the Spirit as such—but it is meaningful to speak of the epistemological relevance of the Holy Spirit. In epistemology we are concerned with the *formal* aspects of knowledge, the forms of the *how* and the forms of the *what* as they arise in our understanding under the impact of the object, whereas in the Spirit we are concerned rather with the *non-formal*, with the given reality or object of our knowledge as it outruns all forms of our understanding, and with the abrupt acts of God through which our understanding of Him arises but which cannot be reduced to forms of our understanding. Thus to erect an epistemology of the Spirit would not only be to presuppose that the knowledge of God is explicable from the side of man, but in effect to substitute some theory of knowledge for the free activity of the Spirit. As knowledge of God actually arises, however, we know that we cannot attribute it to ourselves and know that we can only say something of how it arises by referring beyond ourselves to God's acts upon us—i.e. though it is our knowledge of Him, it is explicable only from the side of God as freely given participation in His self-knowledge. The epistemological relevance of the Holy Spirit lies in the dynamic and transformal aspects of this knowledge.

It is important to remember, as Athanasius used to insist, that the Son of God is the only *Logos* and *Eidos* of Godhead.[1] It is in and through the incarnate Word of God in Jesus Christ that God reveals Himself as Father, Son and Holy Spirit, and is believed and acknowledged in accordance with His divine nature and rationality; it is in and through the incarnate Form of God in Jesus Christ that His Face and Image are revealed and that our human knowledge of Him is shaped and formed through the conformity of our minds to Jesus Christ. Thus by letting our thinking obediently follow the way God Himself has taken in

---

[1] *Contra Arianos*, 3.15; *Ad Serapionem*, 1.19.

Jesus Christ we allow the *basic forms* of theological truth to come to view. That happens, however, only as in the Spirit the being and nature of God is brought to bear upon us so that we think under the compulsion of His Reality. That is the activity of the Holy Spirit whom Jesus spoke of in this connection as the Spirit of Truth.

The Holy Spirit is not cognoscible in Himself, but it is in the Spirit that we are confronted with the ultimate being and presence of God. When that happens there is ἀλήθεια, for truth is the unveiling of what was hidden, the manifestation of the divine Reality—that is why He is called the Spirit of Truth: it is through His agency that Jesus Christ is revealed as the Son of the Father. He does not bear witness to Himself but bears witness to Christ as God and Saviour. He does not show us Himself, but shows us the Face of the Father in the Face of the Son, and shows us the heart of the Son in the heart of the Father. By His very mode of being as Spirit He hides Himself from us so that we do not know Him directly in His own hypostasis, and in His mode of activity as transparent Light He effaces Himself that the one Triune God may shine through Him to us. Yet because it is through Him that the Word of God was made flesh and through Him that the Word continues to be heard and believed, because it is in His Light that we see Light and by His creative operation that we know the unknowable and eternal God, we know Him as no less Lord God than the Father and the Son, who with the Father and the Son together is worshipped and glorified. He is Himself God of God, the Holy Spirit of one substance with the Father and of one substance with the Son, who confronts us in His own Person with the ultimate Godness of God. However, unlike the Son He is not of one substance with us, for He incarnated the Son and did not incarnate Himself, He utters the Word but does not utter Himself, and therefore He directs us through Himself to the one *Logos* and *Eidos* of Godhead in Jesus Christ in accordance with whom all our knowledge of God is formed in our minds, knowledge of the Spirit as well as of the Father and of the Son. That is the self-effacing nature of the Spirit who hides Himself behind the Father in the Son and behind the Son in the Father, but also the enlightening transparence of the Spirit who by throwing His eternal Light upon the Father through the Son and upon the Son in the Father, brings the Being and Reality of God out of His hiddenness to bear upon man, and brings man out of his darkness to have communion with God, in Jesus Christ. He is the creative Agent of God's revelation to us and the creative Agent in our reception and understanding of that revelation, but He is not Himself the Word of that revelation or the Form which it assumes as it proceeds from God and is appropriated by man. He is the living Action and Presence of God in it all, who so relates the divine Word to the human and earthly forms which it assumed in Jesus Christ that in Him we are enabled to meet God face to face, shining in His own uncreated Light and speaking to us personally in His own eternal Word.

Now how are we to relate this to our human modes of knowing, for it is only with our *human* knowledge of God that we can be concerned? Are we to think of this as somehow heightened or spiritualized until it becomes supra-rational or ecstatic? Surely not, for it is the miraculous nature of the Spirit's activity that while He creates in us the ability to know God beyond all creaturely and human capacities this does not involve any suppression of our rational and critical powers. If we are enabled to apprehend God in His own divine nature, it is without having to take our feet off the ground, so to speak, or without having to transcend our human nature in its setting in space and time. In no way are we asked to take leave of our senses or to take irrational leaps—precisely the opposite is the case. Here we have to do with sober, self-critical activity, with careful, controlled judgements, with rational knowledge in its own right. We are concerned with modes of knowledge which have to be questioned and tested as to their real ground in actual knowledge, and with human forms of thought and speech which have to be examined and corrected to see that they are rightly and appropriately related to the realities to which they claim to refer. This is, in fact, the area of the Spirit's relevance to our human knowledge, where modes of knowing are related to being and forms of thought and speech refer to realities beyond themselves, where in order to have knowledge at all we must be able to distinguish what we know from our knowing of it and certainly from what we say of it. It is the area of epistemological diastasis where cognitive and semantic denotation are at work directing us to objective realities and bringing us to think and speak of them under the compulsion of their being upon us.

In all our knowledge, even of created things, where we are concerned with the relation of thought to being, we are up against what is transcendent to thought and always reaches beyond what we are able to specify. If we try to close the gap between the specifiable and the non-specifiable, or between the objectifiable and the objective, we destroy knowledge, and if we make the gap complete we again destroy knowledge and are thrown back upon ourselves. If we reduce everything to forms of thought and speech and so formalize our understanding entirely, we become imprisoned in ourselves and live in abstraction from reality, and if we seek to leave forms behind in an attempt to break through into a non-formal world of being beyond, we grasp nothing and only engage in empty movements of thought. In authentic knowledge, however, we are always in situations where the realities we think break through the frames of thought we construct in order to interpret them, where being will not be shackled by the forms we bring to it, yet where frames and forms of thought are quite indispensable for rational knowledge. We proceed by establishing relations between thought and being but always by rejecting any confusion between them, and since being is the abiding source of all our thought we proceed continually by deepening and clarifying these relations. This does not mean that the relation of thought to being can be reduced to thought or that being is somehow formless in itself and can only be thought when we import forms into it, but rather that thought attains its true forms only as it submits to the masterful impact of being upon it and seeks to be conformed to its inherent rationality, and that thought maintains its integrity as it refuses to equate the forms of thought which it attains in this way with the inherent forms of being.

All this holds good for theology, but here we have to do with the relations of human forms of thought and speech to the divine Being and with modes of knowledge in which we bring our thinking under the compulsion of the inherent rationality of the divine Being. But if in relation to creaturely being we find ourselves up against a source of rational experience that reaches out indefinitely beyond what we can delimit in our forms of thought and speech, so that those forms must break off their precisions and specifications in order to point beyond to what cannot be reduced to our control in this way, how much more is that true of our relation with God, the eternal and infinite Source of all being, who by His very nature is greater than what we can ever think? Here also it is true that we would only engage in empty movements of thought if we sought to pass beyond all form into some realm of undifferentiated and non-conceptual experience of God, for that could only be a leap into irrationality. Even though God transcends all that we can think and say of Him, it still holds good that we cannot have experience of Him or believe in Him without conceptual forms of understanding—as Anselm used to say: *fides esse nequit sine conceptione*.[1] This then is the specific domain of the Spirit in theological knowledge, for by His power and enlightenment we think and speak directly of God in and through the forms of our rational experience and articulation and we do that under the direction and control of the inner rationality of the divine Being, the eternal *Logos* and *Eidos* of Godhead. To use Anselmic language once again, here we are up against the *Suprema Veritas*, or the *Ratio Veritatis* of God Himself, which we cannot reduce to the *veritates* or *rationes* of our understanding even though it is only through them that we know God. It is only through the Spirit of Truth that such *trans-formal* experience is possible, for it is by His Power that we are enabled to know beyond ourselves and to distinguish what we know from our knowing of it, so that our knowing of Him falls under the continual informing and shaping of what He makes known of Himself. This is knowledge with a transcendence in form and an indefinite range of enlightenment beyond anything else in our experience, in which our thinking becomes objectively rooted in the eternal Word in the Being of

[1] *De Concordia*, iii, *Opera Omnia* (edit. by F. S. Schmitt), II, p. 271, 7-8.

God and acquires out of that Word a basic conceptuality that does not vary with the many forms of man's self-centred and objectifying modes of thought.

Before we go on to be more precise about the place and activity of the Spirit in the epistemological ground of theology, it may be helpful to draw together in a series of statements the main aspects of the doctrine of the Spirit that bear upon our subject.

(I) The Holy Spirit is the Lord God acting out of the free ground of His own divine Being, in the total sovereignty and power of His Presence. Toward the creation the Spirit is the living presence of God in which He is free to be with His creation, not only acting upon it from the creative side of the Creator-creature relationship but acting within the creature-Creator relationship in order to realize the Godward relation of the creature and so to establish it in its life before God. His special function is thus to bring to completion the creative purpose of God. This lordly freedom of the Spirit means that the creature does not have a continuity in relation to God that belongs to the creature in itself, for this is continuously given and sustained by the presence of the Spirit within the creation bringing creaturely relations to their *telos* in God. This makes impossible for us any notion of a mutual correlation between the creature and the Creator.

(II) In relation to the creation of human being the Spirit is God in His personal presence to the creature freely actualizing within it corresponding personal relations, opening it up toward God within its knowing and loving, creating within it capacity for God, and so fulfilling knowledge of Himself within the creature. This takes place on the ground of the inner personal relations of the Holy Trinity and in the fellowship of Father, Son and Holy Spirit in all the operations of creation and revelation, but since it is only by the Son or Word that God has brought creation into being and revealed Himself within it, it takes place only in the inseparable relation of the Spirit to the Word. It belongs to the mode of His being and the nature of His operation that the Holy Spirit does not come in His own Name but in the Name of the Son, and that we cannot think of His creative and revealing work in human being independently from that of the Son or apart from the incarnation of the Word. Here we are concerned with a two-fold doctrine: an ontological relation between all men and the human nature of the Son, for the incarnation of the Word by whom all things are made posits a creative relation between Jesus Christ and all human being; and a personal presence of the Holy Spirit to all men sustaining and consummating their creaturely relations with God through the Word, opening them up in their human being and life for communion with God, in fellowship with the revealing and reconciling work of Jesus Christ. Hence we are prevented from entertaining a notion of the Spirit as the rational principle that informs all things with order or imparts to human being form from out of Himself which can be brought to expression within the cosmos as its inherent entelechy. Rather must we think of the Spirit as actualizing within creation its bond of union with the *Logos*, so that it is through the power of the Spirit that human minds are informed with the Word and enlightened with the Truth as through the same Spirit they are united to Christ on the ground of His atoning and renewing work. Thus it is through the Son that the Spirit comes, from the Son that He shines forth, to the Son that He bears witness, and in the Spirit that God is known and man is recreated after His Image in Jesus Christ.

(III) While the Holy Spirit does not inform us with His own Form but through Himself with the Form of the Word, since in His mode of Being and activity as Spirit He hides Himself from us, yet in Himself He brings us to participate in the communion of the Father and the Son, and therefore in the inexhaustible Truth of the divine Being. He is the Spirit that goes forth from God and returns to God, who brings God to bear directly upon us and lifts us up to experience the undiluted acts of God Almighty. Yet He is never other than God, for He is God who, without ceasing to be what He eternally is in His ineffable majesty and sublimity, is free to condescend to mortal men on earth and, unlimited by their creaturely incapacity for Him, to present Himself to them in His own transcendent Being and Reality, and so to emancipate them from imprisonment in themselves and their weakness and to raise them up to partake of His creative and eternal Life. Thus with the coming of the Spirit to us the Being of God Almighty, the Maker of heaven and earth, breaks through the distance between the creature and the Creator, shines through all the intermedia of our creaturely existence and knowledge, disclosing Himself to us personally. Therefore, for us to be in the Spirit means to come up against God in the most absolute and ultimate sense, in His sheer Godness, to meet and experience Him in His immutable Reality who, by being the Lord God and by giving Himself to us as our God, lays absolute and exclusive claim upon our worship and love and obedience. Because the Spirit is the active and living presence of this One and Only God, He resists all our attempts to be independent of Him or to get alongside of Him or to manipulate Him for our own ends. Hence in all our knowing of God the Spirit of Truth is God's striving with us in our masterful ways, the active opposition of His Reality to our self-centred conceptions, in which He convicts us of falsifying the truth and of confounding Him with our own subjective states, and in which He distinguishes Himself from our spirits, and His divine activity from all our creative spirituality. The presence of the Holy Spirit means, therefore, that while God reveals Himself to us within the subject–object structures of our existence in space and time He encounters us always as the Lord in the implacable objectivity of His divine Being, objecting to our objectifying modes of thought and imparting Himself to us in accordance with the modes of His own self-revealing through the Word.

(IV) The Holy Spirit is God in His freedom not only to be present to us but to dwell with us and to operate within us and so to realize from the side of our inward being the response of truth toward God. Hence when He fills us with Himself it is in order to redeem us from our in-turned and in-grown existence, and when He possesses our subjectivities it is in order to turn our spirits outward and upward to God, and so to restore to us the true centre of our being and knowing in Him. The Holy Spirit interiorizes the knowledge of God within us, but He does this by actualizing within us God's own witness to Himself. The Holy Spirit is the eternal Communion of the Father and the Son and therefore when He is sent into our hearts by the Father in the Name of the Son we are made partakers with the Son in His

Communion with the Father and thus of God's own self-knowledge. As the Spirit of Truth, He is the self-communication and the self-speaking of the divine Being dwelling within us who renews our minds, articulates God's Word within our understanding, leads us into all truth, so that through the Spirit we are converted from ourselves to thinking from a centre in God and not in ourselves, and to knowing God out of God and not out of ourselves.

This activity of the Spirit is not independent of that of the Son but is carried through only in fellowship with His saving work in which He exchanged His riches for our poverty that we might exchange our poverty for His riches. Christ suffered for our sins, the Just for the unjust, that He might bring us to God. God made Him to be sin for us, who knew no sin, that we might be made the righteousness of God in Him. The Holy Spirit so works that saving exchange within our lives that He produces from our side its counterpart in the renunciation of ourselves for Christ: I am crucified with Christ (as St. Paul expressed it), nevertheless I live, yet not I but Christ lives in me. Thus through the blood of Christ and the power of the Holy Spirit we are cleansed and renewed in the depth of our conscience, so that *con-science* becomes a knowing together with Christ and with one another in Him, and always out of a centre in Him. In this way the work of the Spirit is correlated to the substitutionary work of Christ, for with His reconciliation He works communion and with His emancipation of ourselves from ourselves He lifts us above and beyond ourselves to find the truth of our being in God. The Holy Spirit operates within us, but in order to turn us inside out. He is at work to realize the Godward side of our life, and to direct us in all our being and knowing away from our own subjectivity to the objective Reality of God's own Being and Word. Indeed, it is through the Holy Spirit that our relations with the objective Reality of God are brought to their *telos*.

II

We have now marked out the area in our human knowledge where we must speak of the relevance of the Holy Spirit, and have also drawn together the principal elements in the doctrine of the Spirit that bear upon our knowledge of God. What are we to say, then, about the propriety and activity of the Spirit in the epistemological ground of this knowledge?

(1) We begin with the all-important relation of our cognitive and semantic acts to the divine Being. It will be recalled that in all knowledge we are concerned with a relation of knowing and speaking to being, and that there must be real diastasis between them if we are to have knowledge at all, for knowledge would never arise or would simply cease if there were an outright disjunction or an outright identity between them. Now here we are up against something of far-reaching importance. It is impossible to reduce to thought how thought is related to being, else all we are left with is mere thought; it is likewise impossible to state in statements how statements are related to being without substituting mere statements for relation to being—nevertheless, in authentic knowledge *being shows through*.[1] Even if we are unable to say how it ultimately happens, a relation takes place in which there is a disclosure of being from beyond our forms of thought and speech and which we must distinguish from our thinking and speaking. Of course, it is possible for us to obstruct such a disclosure as we do when we damage our cognitive and semantic relations with being, but the forms of our thought and speech which we use in knowledge must point beyond themselves if they are to be instruments of actual knowledge.

It is right here that we discern the propriety of the Holy Spirit in our knowledge of God, for the Spirit is the presence of the transcendent Being of God. Apart from the Spirit we would not break through to the divine Being, or rather the divine Being would not break through to us in His reality as Being and thus in His distinction from our thought and speech of Him. It must be granted that in all knowledge there is a distinction between the specifiable and the non-specifiable, or the objectifiable and the non-objectifiable; but what we have here is not just a special instance of that. Here we have to do with the Spirit of God in

[1] Cf. Plato, *Cratylus*, 433 B, 438 D.

His utter sublimity and exaltedness and here we are up against the ultimate Source and Ground of being beyond all being, and therefore we are at the one point where the necessity for epistemological diastasis between the reality we know and our knowing of it becomes supremely compelling. Thus even as the object of our knowledge the Being of God remains utterly transcendent and the Truth of God retains His own Majesty. It is in fact under the Lordship of the Spirit that we learn what objectivity in knowledge really is.

On the one hand, then, the Holy Spirit through His presence brings the very Being of God to bear upon us in our experience, creating the relation to the divine Being which knowledge of God requires in order to be knowledge; but on the other hand, the Spirit through His ineffable and self-effacing nature reinforces the impossibility of our conceiving in thought and expressing in speech how our thought and speech are related to God, so that our thoughts and statements by referring infinitely beyond themselves break off before Him in wonder, adoration and silence, that God may be All in all. Through the Spirit empirical relation to the divine Being takes place and within it we are given intuitive knowledge of God, but the mode of our relation to Him and the mode of our knowledge of Him must be in accordance with His nature as *Spirit*, and therefore even though we have empirical relation to Him and intuitive knowledge of Him, they are not amenable to the kind of control which we exercise in relation to creaturely objects. It is rather we who fall under the overwhelming presence of the divine Being and come under the control of His Spirit in our experience and knowledge of Him.

(II) We now turn to the fact that the Being of God *acts* upon us in our knowledge of Him, for the Spirit is the active and creative presence of God to us. Although we cannot relate our thought and speech to the Being of God, far less state in statements how they can be related, nevertheless that relation takes place through the *action* of God, for it is only by God that we know God. That is the activity of the Spirit in the epistemological ground of our knowledge, for in Him we meet God's Being in

His Act and His Act in His Being. Once again, although it may be true that all knowledge rests upon action, this is not just a special instance of that for here we have to do with the creative source of all knowledge and therefore with a different kind of action. This is unique action in which God's own Being is wholly present in His activity so that the given Object of our knowledge is actively at work in our knowing of it, creating from our side a corresponding action in which our own being is committed. That is why theological thinking is essentially a spiritual activity in which we are engaged in a movement that corresponds to the movement of the Spirit and indeed participates in it. It is a form of kinetic thinking in which the reason does not apprehend the truth by sitting back and thinking ideas, but in an act or movement in which it participates in what it seeks to know. Thus in order to know Jesus Christ, the eternal Word became flesh, the Truth of God in historical happening, we must know Him in a way apposite to that divine becoming and happening in space and time, and therefore κατὰ πνεῦμα, as St. Paul said. This is what Kierkegaard used to call 'the leap of faith', but it would be a grave misunderstanding to think of this as a blind or irrational movement, for it is the very reverse of that.

We may compare this kind of thinking to that in which Einstein engaged in formulating his theory of relativity by abandoning conceptions of space and time reached from a point of absolute rest. Or we may compare it to the heuristic step which the physicist must take in crossing a logical gap between knowledge he already has and knowledge he is yet to gain but which he cannot acquire by inference from what he already knows and which, when he does acquire it, involves a logical reconstruction of what he already knows. Or again, we may want to compare it to Heidegger's leap of thought to open up the original source of being. We direct our questions to existents in order to let their being disclose itself to us, but since being itself is hidden from us and cannot be made the object of direct study we must press our questioning to its utmost limit until it can go no further, i.e. to the very horizon of being. At that point, we have to engage in a leap of thought beyond all causal and logical relation, projecting inquiry through and beyond the existence of the questioner himself into the unknown, if the ultimate ground of being is to have any light thrown upon it at all.

None of these comparisons is adequate. In none of them are we concerned with being that really *acts* upon us but only with our own attempts to make being disclose itself. We ourselves have both to pose the questions and to answer them, and since we ourselves always stand behind our questions we are left finally alone with ourselves, without Another to put to us the ultimate question that will carry us beyond ourselves to open up the original source of our being. All we can do, as Heidegger claims, is to take the leap into nothing or into death. But if we are to reckon without God, what is this after all but a meaningless leap into the void? In theology we are certainly engaged in a movement of thought in which we think not from some still point of abstraction but from within the movement of divine revelation: in which we are faced with what is so utterly new that we have to step beyond what we already know in order to apprehend it and can assimilate it into our knowledge only through repentant rethinking of all our presuppositions; and in which we are relentlessly questioned down to the roots of our existence where we have to cease from ourselves and listen if we are to be carried to what is utterly beyond us. But how can this take place unless God Himself, the Ground of our being from beyond our being, acts upon us, not only to give us His own Being as the object of our knowledge, but to be with us and in us and so to realize from our side active relation to the divine Being in which we can be carried beyond ourselves to genuine knowledge of Him? That is what God accomplishes through the living presence and action of His Spirit both from the side of God toward us and from our side toward God. Theological knowledge that is grounded in the activity of the Spirit, who proceeds from God and returns to God, participates in the one movement that can carry man above and beyond himself to real knowledge of the divine Being, the movement, that is, of God's own self-revelation and self-knowledge. It is because God is at work through His Spirit enclosing man within the circle of that movement that our questioning and answering, our knowing and speaking of Him, may reach a fruition which we could never give them.

That it is not man but God Himself who activates and sustains the relation between human knowing and His divine Being is of immense importance for theological epistemology, for in man's knowledge of God we have to face the hard fact of man's estrangement from God and his enmity to Him. Here, then, where we have to reckon with a damaged relation between human knowing and the divine Being, and all the misunderstanding, opaqueness and darkness that result from it, our one hope rests in the fact that any synthesis between our knowing and God's Being is exclusively God's act. That means that knowledge of God is possible only on the ground of reconciliation between man and God which He establishes, and never through any synthesis which we human beings may seek to achieve. Were it not for the mercy of God in which He throws the co-ordinating circle of His grace around all our contradictions and misunderstandings and sends His Spirit to heal the breach between our knowing and His divine Being we would never come to know Him at all, but could only fall back into darkness and futility. But true knowledge of God may result, and does result, when we let our knowing fall under His reconciling grace and under the co-ordinating action of His Spirit.

(III) The divine Being who acts upon us in our knowledge of Him is not dark or mute Being but *eloquent Being*: God speaking in Person, God uttering or speaking Himself. We have already noted that God's Being is His Being-in-His-Act, and His Act is His Act-in-His-Being. Now we have to take a further step, and note that His Being and His Word are related in the same way, for His Act is His Word and His Word is His Act. In His own essence God is articulate Being—Word is not incidental to God, nor some detachable emanation from Him, but His own Being in action, for in His Word God communicates not something of Himself, nor just something about Himself, but Himself. His own eternal Being is wholly and inseparably involved in His Word, and His Word is backed up by and filled with His Being. This is where we are concerned with the propriety of the Spirit to the Father and the Son, for it is through the Spirit of God that He utters His Word, and through the Spirit that the Word comes to us as dynamic communication and creative event. The Holy Spirit who is the consubstantial Communion of the Father and the Son in the Trinity, is the Spirit through whom the Word was made flesh in the hypostatic union of the divine and human natures in the Person of the Son, but it is the same Spirit through whom we have union with Christ and partake of the communion between the Father and the Son and the Son and the Father.

The Spirit and the Word are inseparably related in the Being and Act of God, yet are distinct both in God and in our knowledge of Him. This is not a distinction, however, between the Spirit as inner Word and the Son as outer Word, nor between the Spirit as subjective Word and the Son as objective Word, for there is only one Word which the Spirit utters in God in one way and in our hearts in another way. In the inner personal relations of the Holy Trinity the Spirit utters the Word in His distinction from the Father and the Spirit, and within our knowledge of God, the Spirit in His own distinction from the Father and the Son utters not Himself but the Word. The distinction of the Spirit from the Word means that the Word of God remains eternally Word and does not disappear into Spirit, yet the inseparable relation of Word and Spirit means that the kind of speaking that takes place in God is appropriate to His nature as Spirit, and is the speaking of the Spirit. On the other hand, the inseparable relation of the Spirit to the Word in the Being of God means that the speaking of the Spirit in our hearts is entirely distinct from the activity of our spirit even though through His speaking within us He makes our spirit articulate in the Word of God.

There are several elements here to be stressed and drawn out.

(a) The Word of God has eternal Reality as Word in God's own Being, for He eternally utters Himself, and is in Himself the Word He utters. The Word is not just the form that the shining of God's Light or the going forth of His Spirit takes in the *opera Trinitatis ad extra* but is eternally in the depth of the divine Being what it is as Word towards us. That is what Anselm spoke of as the *locutio intima apud Summam Substantiam*.[1] Through the Spirit

---

[1] *Monologion*, 10–12, *Opera Omnia* (edit. by F. S. Schmitt), II, pp. 24ff.

that 'intimate locution' of God is related to the creation in the bringing of things out of nothing into being and in the sustaining of them as created realities before God which somehow have a *locutio rerum* embedded in them answering to the creative *locutio* in God (we continue here to use Anselm's way of speaking); but through the Spirit the 'intimate locution' of God is related in another way to our human knowledge of God which is made to enshrine an *intima locutio* by way of rational response to the Word uttered by the Spirit in the Holy Scriptures. This is surely another way of stating Calvin's doctrine of the *testimonium internum Spiritus Sancti* which is not some subjective or inner word of the heart but a speaking within the heart by the Spirit of the one eternal Word intimate to the Being of God which we hear through the Scriptures. That is to say, through the Spirit and the Word God speaks to us, articulates Himself within our minds, and makes Himself understood by us in accordance with His self-revelation, so that the essential conceptuality inherent in our knowledge of Him is conferred upon it from the 'intimate locution' in God and is objectively grounded in His divine Being—and is not, therefore, just construction out of man's own independent interpretation.

(b) It follows from this that the co-ordinating principle of theological knowledge does not lie in theological activity itself but in the speaking of the Word by the Spirit and in our participation in the Word through the Spirit. We cannot relate our knowing to the Being of God, or the actuality of our knowledge to the Truth of God by thinking our own way into God—that would be tantamount to substituting the movement of our own spirit for that of the Spirit of God and to erecting our own word into the Word of God. Theological knowledge must take the road from God to man before it takes the road from man to God. Thus theology does not know God by virtue of its own ideas and concepts or by the inner power of its own dialectic and spirituality, but only in response to God's Word, only in the recognition of His truth, and only under the leading of His Spirit, and therefore only in humble acknowledgment that its own thought is inadequate to its object, that its own ideas and concepts are unfit of themselves to express or convey knowledge of God, and only in thanksgiving and wonder at the mercy of God who in spite of all is pleased to accept our service and to confer upon our thought, as it falls under the action of His Spirit and Word, the truth of His own Being. By its very nature, therefore, theological activity has its objective basis not in itself but in God, and must never presume to find its truth in itself but only in Him. A genuine theology will always be open to the questioning and speaking of the Spirit so that it may never become an undertaking on its own but may ever be meek and obedient service to God's own testimony to Himself.

(c) This relation of theological knowledge to the objective Word or 'intimate locution' in the Being of God means that its basic statements can be made only in the form of *recognition-statements*. The basic act of knowledge is not creative or inventive in which the human reason forms conceptions of its own by positing an object before it, so that in this way it establishes itself as the basis of reality by building a world of reality on its own inventions and achievements. The basic act of knowledge is one in which the reason acts in accordance with the nature of the given object, that is, acknowledges and recognizes it, so that it attains its essential conceptuality as it lets its thinking follow the inherent rationality of the given. In natural science, for example, the reason does not invent geometrical patterns and impose them upon nature in the form of crystals which it posits in this way; rather does it follow as closely as it can the mathematical structure of nature by letting it disclose itself to the reason in order that it may think in accordance with it and thus understand it. In this way natural science operates with recognition-statements arising out of its reflection of the rationality of the universe.

This is even more true of theological activity for in it the human reason finds itself posited with a given reality that is not a dumb or inert object of knowledge but the Holy Spirit speaking the Word of God and in that Word presenting the very Being of God as the creative source and objective ground of our knowledge of Him. Thus the basic act of theological knowledge arises by way of acknowledgment and reflection of the self-articulation of

God brought to bear upon us by His Spirit, in which our reason develops a profound conceptuality that derives from and is rooted in the eternal Reality of God. Hence theological statements are formed as through the speaking of the Spirit the objective Word of God calls forth language from us which is sustained and actualized in relation to God by the same Spirit as the mode of God's communication with men, and as through the obedient response of our minds to the Spirit we seek to let our answering word take the form which it must take under the imprint of God's Word if it is to be correlated to that Word and be the medium of its recognition among men. True theological statements, then, are formed as we allow them to enshrine an 'intimate locution' which echoes or reflects the 'intimate locution' in the divine Being and which can only be conferred upon them through the operation of the Spirit of Truth—in this way they are no less and ultimately no more than recognition-statements which, though formed under the determination of their given object, by their very nature point beyond themselves to the Word of God as their sole justification and truth.

(iv) The Holy Spirit is at work in our knowledge of God, not only in creating and calling forth from us forms of thought and speech answering to the *Logos* and *Eidos* of Godhead, but in shining the divine Light or sounding the divine Word through those forms of thought and speech, so that God may disclose Himself to us not apart from them but *through* them. In this respect the Holy Spirit has a double work to do, in *creation* and *revelation*. As we have already seen, the Spirit is God in His freedom both to bring creaturely realities into being distinct from Himself and to be present to them in such a way as to realize their relation to Himself as the Creator. But the Spirit of God is also the personal presence and action of God to the human creature both to give him rational life in sustained relation to Himself and to open his mind to receive and understand God's self-revelation and so to respond to Him in faith and love. In the fulfilment of this second work, the Holy Spirit makes use of creaturely realities which God has made as the media of divine revelation yet in such a way that in his response to it man's knowledge of God does not terminate on the media but on the Being of God Himself.

That is to say, God reveals Himself to man not, as it were, in His naked majesty, but in the medium of the creaturely existence to which man belongs in space and time, and uses the sign-world of inter-human communication in order to communicate Himself to man. Thus He determines, within the created world, within man's life and history, and within the subject-object structures of his existence, certain facts and events as the signs or the mediate objectivities of His revelation, yet in the living presence and power of His Spirit God is Himself personally present in the midst directing man through these determinations to immediate, intuitive knowledge of Himself in His own ultimate Objectivity and Reality. This sign-world which God has appointed and uses in our mediate knowledge of Him comprises the whole history of His covenant relations with His people as fulfilled in the incarnation of His Word in Jesus Christ, and it comprises the whole realm of the biblical revelation with its created forms of thought and speech and worship called forth from human life under the inspiration of the Holy Spirit and appointed as the medium which He continues to use in the revelation of God to man. Thus God still comes to us clothed in the historical and biblical forms of His revelation which (whether B.C. or A.D.) direct us to Jesus Christ in the centre, for it is in Him that God has objectified Himself for our human knowing, but through the power and presence of the Holy Spirit we are enabled to meet God and know Him directly and immediately in Jesus Christ, and under the compulsion of His Being and Truth upon us in Christ to formulate in our own statements our understanding of Him—yet all this only within our human existence and history and their rational, linguistic and social structures. In this way God shuts us up, as it were, to knowledge of Him in and through the human and worldly and historical forms which His revelation has assumed and so excludes from us any possibility of non-objective knowledge, and at the same time through the presence of His Spirit He encounters us immediately in His own personal Being as Supreme Subject, and thus in all His ultimate objectivity as Lord God.

However, since God mediates this revelation of Himself only through created realities and through forms of thought and speech that are taken from our own structured existence in the world of space and time and are therefore correlated to these created realities, these creaturely realities and forms of thought and speech must be interpreted beyond their this-worldly reference if they are to be the medium in which God reveals *Himself*. In all our knowledge of God we make use of human and earthly signs and forms, cognitive, linguistic, liturgical, social, historical, etc., but in themselves these forms are quite opaque as far as their reference to God is concerned. Because they are taken from man's intra-mundane existence, and from within the subject–object structure of his relations with the world of nature and other human beings, in themselves they are merely expressions of earthly and natural and human activity that reveal not God but man in his creaturely existence. If they really are to serve their purpose they must be made to point beyond themselves to the divine realities they are used to signify and must undergo a profound shift in meaning if they are actually to signify them. Thus even the biblical statements and all the forms of signification in thought and speech they involve can be interpreted in their human reference as expressing the attitudes and thoughts and the time-conditioned and space-conditioned limitations of their human authors, and when left to themselves can only be interpreted in that way. That is to say, we interpret them only in terms of their mediate and not their ultimate objectivity in God's own self-revelation. Now this is precisely where the activity of the Holy Spirit comes in, and His propriety to the Word of God, for He is at work in all His divine ineffability and transparence, who through His speaking of the eternal Word and shining of the uncreated Light so relates the human and worldly forms of divine revelation to God Himself that they become diacoustic and diaphanous media through which God discloses Himself to us in His own Word and Reality and makes us capable of knowing Him beyond ourselves. Apart from this work of the Holy Spirit all the forms of revelation remain dark and opaque but in and through His presence they become translucent and transparent.

Applied to our theological knowledge, it is in the epistemological reference of the Spirit that we find the answer to our most
difficult questions. How is it that we think by means of our human
thinking what utterly transcends our thought? How is it that
human beings, by means of human language, have come to speak
of what is ineffable? How can we through human words which
are correlated to created realities speak truly of the Supreme Being
who transcends them altogether? This is what takes place through
the operation of the Holy Spirit who relates the divine Being to
our forms of thought and speech and realizes the relation of our
forms of thought and speech to the Truth of God—what cannot
be done by our thinking or stating is done by His *action* as Spirit
of God, as He lets the eternal Light of God shine through Himself
into our minds and enlightens our understanding that we may
hear and discern God and think and speak truly of Him.

This means that in our handling of the Holy Scripture we have
to respect its *perspicuity*, and must not interpret biblical statements
or the forms of thought they express merely as they are in themselves as linguistic or logical facts, nor only in their subjective
reference to their human authors—important as that is to discover
their proper intention—but ultimately in their objective reference
to God, and as they should be in the Supreme Truth, i.e. in
a dimension of rationality and objectivity that reaches out far
beyond them into the divine Being and is backed up by His creative
Word and Spirit. This also means that in our theological activity
we must learn to discern that the truth of the realities is independent of the statements we make in signifying them, and that our
statements are more true the more open they are to the ultimate
Truth. Indeed that *openness* to the Truth of God is the specific
nature of their adequacy and is the mode of their correspondence
to the Truth. Thus true statements about God have a dimension
of depth which they acquire through pointing to the infinite and
eternal Truth of God who far transcends all our thoughts and
statements about Him.

Theological statements operate, then, with what we may call
open concepts—concepts which, to be sure, must be closed on our
side, for we have to formulate them as carefully and exactly as

we can, but which on God's side are open (and therefore apposite) to the infinite objectivity and inexhaustible reality of the divine Being. That is to say, the kind of conceptuality with which we operate in theology is one in which our acts of cognition are formed from beyond them by the reality disclosed so that the content of what is revealed constantly bursts through the forms we bring to it in order to grasp it. This can happen only under the power of the Spirit, as He presses upon us from the side of the divine Being. The Spirit is thus the act of God upon us which keeps our concepts or cognitive forms open, so that our thought and speech are stretched out beyond themselves toward the inexhaustible nature of the divine Being. Apart from this impact of the Spirit upon us, the forms of our thought and speech become quite obscure and indeed may even become a form of obstruction to the divine revelation or a means of suppressing the truth through the transmutation of knowledge into our own constructs.

It is important to see that open concepts are not irrational because they are open, for to be open vis-à-vis the eternal God is the true mode of their rationality, prescribed for them by the nature of the divine Object of knowledge—they would in fact be most imprecise and inaccurate if they were not open in this way. At the same time, their openness indicates the limits of our human inquiry beyond which we cannot rationally go, or the limitation of our powers to put into words our understanding of the divine rationality which will not be restricted or confined within our finite formulations. Nevertheless, within these limits we may and indeed we must probe as deeply as we can and seek to make clear the rationality which we are given to apprehend. It is for this purpose that we have to use open concepts which by their very nature do not describe, delimit or define the Reality we seek to understand, but which we employ as media through which we allow our minds to come under the compulsion of the Reality so that we think of it only as we are forced to, and let them be opened out more and more in accordance with its richness and range in enlightenment. Thus the very 'inadequacy' of these concepts to their objects is essential to their truth, for they would not be true unless they pointed far beyond any 'adequacy' they have to the infinite and eternal God. Without the Spirit, we have no opening to the transcendent Being, but through the Spirit our concepts are opened in such a way that He is accessible to us—if we close these concepts in order to give them the kind of precision apposite only to concepts we develop in knowledge of determinate realities, then we smother knowledge of God and evade His Reality. Knowledge of God in the Spirit is profoundly conceptual, rational knowledge in its own right, knowledge in which we are carried right over to what transcends us, yet which is apposite to the nature of God as *Spirit*.

(v) Knowledge of God takes place not only within the rational structures but also within the personal and social structures of human life, where the Spirit is at work as *personalizing Spirit*. As the living presence of God who confronts us with His personal Being, addresses us in His Word, opens us out toward Himself, and calls forth from us the response of faith and love, He rehabilitates the *human subject*, sustaining him in his personal relations with God and with his fellow creatures.

Within his subject-object relations where he is concerned with things, the human subject easily falls under the pressure of determinate objects and their mechanical connections and tends to become impersonal, or in reaction to the menace of this objectivism he tends to subdue everything to his own subjectivity and so to get locked up in himself. Then in order to secure himself he objectifies his own subjective states and conditions and projects them above and around him as his real world, thus shutting himself off from authentic objectivity and perverting his own true nature as a subject vis-à-vis other subjects (or 'voluntary' objects) as well as determinate (or 'involuntary') objects. Now it is in his knowledge of God where through the Spirit man learns what objectivity really is, by coming up against the unyielding objectivity of the Lord God before which his own objectified constructions are shattered, that he is emancipated from the prison-house of his own in-turned subjectivity, and is made free for genuinely objective experience. At the same time here where through the Holy Spirit man encounters His Creator in His personal Being and Majesty, and therefore in His inviolable Subject-ivity, man is delivered from the threat of impersonalizing objectivism and determinism, and is set on his feet before God, and therefore also before his fellows, as free and spontaneous subject capable of personal relations with others. That is to say, in being made open for God in his thinking and knowing and loving, man is also made open for experience of all that is other than himself whether in subject–subject or in subject–object relations. This is made possible under the impact of God's own transcendent Spirit upon him, for through participation in that Spirit, he acquires a personal transcendence of his own and is rehabilitated as human subject.

This is the personalizing work of the Holy Spirit who, coming from the inter-personal Communion of the Holy Trinity, establishes divine communion among us by reconciling us with God and by creating within the personal and social structures of our human life the Community of the redeemed whose personal relations with God and with one another are sustained through His own creative presence. Theological knowledge takes place, and theological statements are enunciated, within this Community where human beings are made open to God, and to one another before Him. It follows that theological statements are to be understood as correlated also with their human subjects, as well as with their given object, not only because those subjects formulate them but because their Object, the divine Subject, posits them as subjects by addressing them personally and claiming from them personal responses. Thus although theological statements take their rise from a centre in God and not in ourselves, the very nature of the divine Object makes it impossible for us to abstract them from the personal and community setting in which they take place without damaging their mode of reference and indeed without falsifying them.

A distinction may be drawn here between a 'judgement' and a 'proposition'. A judgement is what we do in thinking, or what takes place within a single mind, even if it assumes dialectical form in question and answer, and the ultimate decision it involves is given from within that mind. A proposition, however, takes place within the relations of objectivity between two or more subjects where the objectivity of one subject encounters the objectivity of another, and where the ultimate decision is not taken in the isolation of a single mind, but in the dependence of one mind on another or other minds, as together they come under the compulsive reality of what is given in common to them. Now certainly in the formulating of theological statements judgements are involved, but they are not, or ought not to be, the expression of private opinions. By their very nature theological statements involve propositional relations with God and propositional relations between human subjects—i.e. they are correlated with God Himself as the prime Subject, and with the collective subjectivity of the Church. They take place, so to speak, within historical conversation between God and His people, as through the Spirit God's Word continues to be uttered, and in the Communion of the Spirit conjoint hearing and understanding take place; they emerge out of the Church's obedient acknowledgment from age to age of the divine Self-revelation in Jesus Christ and are progressively deepened and clarified through the Church's worship and dialogue and repentant rethinking within the whole communion of saints. Hence the more ecumenical they are, i.e. the more they are formulated within the openness of the members of the whole Community to one another before God, the more likely they are to escape distortion through false in-turned subjectivity and to be properly open toward God. Although theological statements are correlated with the Community, that is nevertheless subsidiary, for it is not the Church but God Himself who is the Object of their reference.

However, this subsidiary correlation of theology with the Church, essential and inescapable as it is, may easily fall a prey to the self-cultivated subjectivity of the times, when the Church instead of pointing away from itself to God and letting the Word of God sound through it to the world, seeks to re-interpret the Word of God to suit contemporary thought and culture. The temptation is not difficult to understand. The Church must employ the language of the people to which it ministers from age to age; but language is the medium of a people's historical self-consciousness, the means of its creative achievements and

self-expression, and the transmitter of its culture. In its proclamation of the Gospel to some nation or society the Church enters into
a dialogue with that nation or society through the very language it
uses. But the Church is also aware of the fact that it cannot fulfil
its mission unless it allows the Gospel to create among men a
medium in their life and culture in which its meaning may be
reflected and its message can take root in history. But how easy
it is for the Church in its mission to become so assimilated itself
to the realm of meaning enshrined in a people's language, that
instead of serving the Word of God in its critical and creative
impact upon men it becomes the servant of contemporary thought
and culture, and that its theology instead of being primarily co-
ordinated with the living God becomes primarily co-ordinated
with the cultivated subjectivities of the times. Indeed, the more
'successful' a Church is and the more it develops a culture among
the people to whom it ministers, the more it yields to the temptation to erect that culture (in which it assimilates the subjectivity
of the people and its own subjectivity together) into a masterful
realm of meaning on its own, detached from the reality to which
it claims to refer. It is not difficult then for such a Church to
transfer the locus of authority from the Word and Truth of God
to its own collective subjectivity, and to identify the Spirit of
God with its own spirit.

That is the immense danger against which the Church must
ever be on its guard in disciplined self-criticism and in the relentless testing of its thought and speech about God to make sure that
they really are about God, deriving from His Word and not simply
from itself. Yet this is not something that can be achieved merely
by method, no matter how rigorous and scientific, for it is only
by divine *action* that man's thought may be related to God's Truth
and his speech may actually refer to God's Being. The Church can
only cast itself in constant prayer upon the Holy Spirit, for He
alone can emancipate it from imprisonment in itself or deliver its
mind from being engrossed in its own subjectivity by confronting
it with the implacable Objectivity of the divine Subject, and call
forth from it a faithful response to the divine self-revelation. He
alone can let God's Word break through to it and sustain the

answering thought and speech of the Church until they are brought really to terminate upon God Himself.

At this point the relevance of the Spirit to our knowledge of God is seen to be sharply eschatological—it lies in His *critical action* through which theological formulations are brought under the judgement of the divine Reality to which they refer so that, though enunciated within the rational and linguistic, personal and social structures of space and time, they may become transparent frames of signification serving the transcendent God instead of being opaque media in which we are flung back finally upon ourselves. Then also it is seen that the given object of the Church's knowledge is really God's own divine Being and Act and not something that passes over into the subjective states of the Church's experience or into the mediate objectivities of its historical involvement with the world. The Spirit of Truth remains abroad in the world convicting of sin, righteousness and judgement; but He is also the personal presence of God who directs us through the witness of the Holy Scripture, and its faithful exposition, to Jesus Christ the incarnate Word of God, guiding us to know the Father in accordance with the way His revelation has taken in the Son, enabling us in our knowing to distinguish the Truth of God from our knowing it, and so to live ever out of Christ and not out of ourselves.

V POSTSCRIPT

8

Theological Persuasion[1]

Persuasion is the ability to win the agreement of those from whom we differ about something, but when we ask how this is done a distinction may be drawn. We may persuade people by convincing their minds and bringing them to assent to what we say, or we may persuade them by moving their feelings and evoking from them the response we desire. In both cases persuasion induces a belief and leads to a commitment, but in the former the controlling factor is a rational judgement rather than an emotive reaction. It is with the first that theological persuasion is principally concerned, but the second has a significant if subsidiary role to play in it as well. Persuasion of this kind would appear to presuppose that communication involves a triadic relation, that there is an inherent rationality in the nature of things, and that we are psychologically averse to change.

In normal acts of communication, in ordinary or scientific activity, we use language with a semantic intention: that is, not so much to express our minds as to refer other minds to something beyond ourselves. While our linguistic and conceptual forms may be communicated directly to other minds, intuitable realities are not directly communicable: we may point them out or refer to them through accepted signs or acquired designations in the hope that others will perceive or apprehend them also, but unless that takes place communication has not achieved its end. Communication takes place between minds that are directed to the same or similar objects and so is necessarily indirect through a triadic relationship, in which one mind directs another mind to an object

[1] Reprinted from *Common Factor*, No. 5, 1968, pp. 47-57.

by referring to it, and in which the other mind by following through the reference to the object understands the intention of the first mind.

This presupposes the rationality of the medium and the context in which communication takes place: that is, not only an intelligible language but an intelligible subject-matter. The things about which we speak to one another must be capable of rational apprehension and of semantic designation. This is something that we assume and operate with in ordinary experience and in science, without attempting to explain it. If the nature of things were not somehow inherently rational they would remain inapprehensible and opaque and indeed we ourselves would not be able to emerge into rationality. It is because things are amenable to rational treatment that we can apprehend them at all; we understand them or get light upon them in so far as we can penetrate into their rationality and develop our grasp of it. Scientific knowledge is that in which we bring the inherent rationality of things to light and expression, as we let the realities we investigate disclose themselves to us under our questioning and we on our part submit our minds to their inherent connections and order. Let it be granted that scientific activity involves a give-and-take between subject and object, and that all knowledge is by way of being a compromise between thought and being; nevertheless it remains an awesome fact that if the nature of things were not inherently rational and apprehensible knowledge could not arise at all, far less communication. We communicate with other minds only when we can get them to submit their thought to the same rationality in things that we have experienced. Thus communication from the very start involves a persuasive element.

This basic persuasiveness is not one-directional, however, especially when we are engaged in a conjoint apprehension of things with other minds that communicate back to us, for in the fuller apprehension that we can have together of the same things there usually takes place a modification in our own apprehension of them and of their rationality. If something is inherently rational, and not merely accidental or surd-like, then it is our fault and not that of the thing itself if we fail to understand it:

we have probably overlaid it with some form of unreality by bringing to its apprehension preconceived ideas that are not appropriate or are wrongly extrapolated from another field of experience. This means that as we seek to penetrate into the rationality of something our inquiry must also cut back into ourselves and into our own presuppositions, for they must be brought into question if we are to be really open to understand the thing concerned out of itself and in accordance with its own nature. In these circumstances persuasion must argue for a reconstruction in our interpretative frame of thought, in order that alien elements may be eliminated from it and new elements assimilated more appropriate to the nature of things we are speaking about.

This brings us to the other factor that we must presuppose in acts of communication and persuasion, that we are psychologically resistant to change in our habits of mind or modification in the structure of our thought, for it is we ourselves, the thinkers who live and work in those frames of thought, who have to be changed with them. Reason is and ought to be the slave of the passions, David Hume said rather outrageously, but in a sense very truly. Feeling is properly a passion, an affection in which we suffer impact or come under attack from something other than ourselves. We may resist it, and this makes it more difficult for us, but only if we go along with it (not necessarily to subscribe to it) may we know and understand it. This is the side of our rationality in which we let ourselves be affected by what we seek to know, we let it impose its own self-witness upon us, and we let ourselves be told by it (an all-important element in *a posteriori* knowledge). Doubtless, this is where there arises a tension between pure science and a masterful technology, the tension between knowing a thing as we follow the clues it provides even when we have to 'torment' it, as Francis Bacon expressed it, and the way of knowing in which we will accept only what we can make and shape according to our own stipulations. Obviously feeling enters into both ways of knowing; but since feeling arises we have to reckon with false feeling, that is, with feeling that has turned back on itself, feeling that is more concerned to express itself and enjoy itself than to act appropriately to what is other than ourselves.

The situation is also complicated by the fact that no rational knowledge is merely *per modum causalitatis*. I cognize this table and typewriter truly when I let myself be compelled by what is there, and think accordingly. When I think thus under the compulsion of the facts I am rational, but I am irrational when I think that the table is a car and the typewriter is a steering-wheel. Yet even though I think rationally as I am compelled to think in accordance with what is actually the case, I am free and not a puppet. There is a moment of the will here, in which I readily submit my mind to the compulsion of the nature of the facts upon me. Because there is this element of freedom, the moment of the will, where I am affected by what is there and where my feelings are roused, I must bring my feelings under disciplined control, lest they are already caught up in some movement or intention alien to the case in question at the moment.

But there is still another element that we have to take into account, the fact that in knowledge and communication, the reality to which we refer cannot be reduced to the forms of our thought and speech about it: being always breaks through the forms we use to apprehend it and will not be confined to them. Unless this were so, we could not really know it, for then we could not distinguish what we know from our knowing of it. It is because knowledge involves this 'relation of transcendent reference', as A. D. Ritchie has called it, that *judgement* plays a very important role in it, in relating the forms of thought and speech to the reality concerned, and in judging their adequacy in the light of it, and thus in developing the appropriate mode of knowing and the apposite mode of speaking about it. This is a difficult element in the act of communication, because there is inevitably a discrepancy between the signitive forms we use and the realities themselves. Hence if communication is to succeed we have to refer to some reality in such a way that we will lead others to form the right judgement in regard to it, for without that they cannot know it or speak about it aright.

In persuasion we are not concerned with 'an artful manipulation of language', in John Stuart Mill's sense, but with getting another to submit his mind to the facts and to think of them in accordance with their nature; yet in order to do that, we must often use a persuasive form of words and that is a real art. Because art is involved persuasion may lapse into sophistry or mere rhetoric. Ultimately we persuade a person of something by convincing him that it is the case, that is, by appealing to its truth or by deceiving him into thinking that what we say of it is true. In persuasion we seek to direct the mind of another to something in such a way that it falls under the compulsion of its reality, and cannot but assent to it. But since we never know *per modum causalitatis*, and cannot communicate what we know directly, the elements of feeling, will, freedom and judgement enter in, and we have to learn how to cope with them faithfully. To persuade someone about something we may have to dig his mind out of a bigoted obsession with a false framework, or seek to wean it from misdirected feeling and heal it of false motivation. Hence in persuasion we have to be able to *move* people and to *convince* them at the same time: that is, to jolt them out of the situation in which their own unrealities and artificialities obscure the truth from them, and to direct them to the reality concerned in such a way that they really see it as it is and as it shows itself out of its own inherent rationality. To *convince* a person of the truth must remain primary and dominant in persuasion, but to move them to adopt the right attitude where a rational judgement can be made in the light of the truth will play a significant if subsidiary role. Whenever we seek to move people through their feelings without leading them to submit their minds to the compulsion of the actual facts, persuasion has lapsed from its integrity, and whenever we abstract language and argument from their proper semantic function and use them in their detachment emotively to evoke the desired reactions or artfully to contrive the acceptance of certain ideas, persuasion has given way to sophistry.

All this applies to theological persuasion as much as to authentic persuasive activity in any other field of experience or knowledge, but in theology there are special factors that have to be taken into account. That is as it should be, for in every field of experience, as John Macmurray has shown us so clearly, we behave rationally when we act in accordance with the nature of object, and allow it to prescribe to us the specific mode of rationality we have to adopt toward it as well as the kind of demonstration appropriate to it. Thus when we take into account the difference in the nature of the object of theological knowledge we discern the difference between 'discovery' and 'revelation'. In natural science, discovery is the heuristic activity (εὑρετικὴ επιστήμη) in which we seek to advance beyond what we know to what is radically new and which we can learn only out of itself. We speak here about 'interrogating' some reality in order to let it 'reveal itself' or 'declare itself' to us; but actually that reality is mute or dumb, for we have not only to frame our own questions to it but to frame its answers to us. In theological knowledge, however, we do not have to do with a mute or dumb reality (that would be an idol) but with One who acts upon us and addresses us in His Word, where the expressions 'reveal itself' and 'declare itself' are really in place. Here we discover what is new through giving our ear to it, and by letting ourselves be told what we could never tell ourselves. This is what is meant by divine revelation. However, both discovery and revelation have to be put to the test to see whether they really are what is claimed, i.e. to see whether it is really discovery or simply a pure invention, and to see whether it is really revelation or merely imagination on our part. At the same time, we have to test the referential relations of our statements to make sure that they are relevant to the realities to which they refer. Here, then, we have a basic common factor, and yet in accordance with the difference in the nature of each kind of reality, a difference between the mode of knowledge that is a form of discovery and the mode of knowledge that is grounded in divine revelation.

This difference affects our acts of communication and persuasion, for here it is God in His Word who forms with us the triadic relation: He takes an active part in our communicating and persuading. We may express this in another way by saying that we are concerned here with a *different kind of rationality* from that which we find embedded in nature, in the geometrical patterns of crystals or the periodicity of the elements, for example. What we discover there is amenable to mathematical treatment and formulation, the kind of rationality which we call 'number', but we cannot think in this way of divine acts which we may apprehend only in accordance with their divine rationality which we call 'Logos' or 'Word'. Confusion between these two would be the equivalent of a 'category-mistake' of a very grave order. If therefore we are to communicate with someone about God and to persuade him in respect of something about Him we must refer him to the divine Logos in order that he may listen to God for himself, for he cannot know God unless he lets Him bear witness to Himself and disclose Himself to him through His own Word.

In theological persuasion, we seek to bring others to the point where they submit their minds to the inherent rationality of the divine revelation. There they must think only as they are compelled to think by the nature of the divine realities themselves, and there they must engage in a critical judgement in which they test the persuasive statements in the light of that to which they refer, and test their own preconceptions to see whether they are importing into what is apprehended something that is not really there or whether they are preventing the apprehension of what is really there but quite new and altogether beyond them. This kind of persuasion cannot achieve its end fully with single individuals, for if God is not merely what I have thought up and projected out there, He is objectively real and universally knowable by others (that is, in so far as they are prepared to know Him in accordance with His own nature). If this is so, my knowing of God will involve not only a private conscience (con-scientia) between myself and God, but a conscience which I share with others knowing Him and in which I submit my private conscience to critical testing in the light of that of others. This will then become part of the test as to whether it is really God I know or an invention of my own.

In natural science we build up knowledge through casting ourselves upon the rationality of the given, and we test the reality and objectivity of our knowledge through the development of its inherent patterns of rationality in a way that not only transcends our experience in the present but proves to be progressively fertile in the light it throws upon other problems and questions. But this testing requires a whole community of verifiers all over the world, for science moves and advances as one, with its internal self-scrutiny and self-criticism, and its own rigorous conscience aroused in it by the compelling claims of reality. So it is with theology. We cannot know God one by one in isolation, for we require the objectivity of one another to help us escape from our own in-turned subjectivities. We learn to know God conjointly and by being assimilated to a community of conscience, ranging across the ages as well as the world, in which our critical judgements are intertwined, and we are subjected to critical questioning and correcting from one another. It is in such a community and continuity of interpretation and understanding that communication takes place, and from it that we seek to persuade others to believe: that is, to induce in others the rational assent which in good conscience we believe they must give if they let their thinking fall under the compelling rationality of the divine Word.

What steps in fact do we normally take in efforts at theological persuasion?

The first and most prevalent, though doubtless the most misused, is *proclamation*, which is not meant to be 'preaching at' people, but to refer them away from themselves to divine and transcendent realities. It is essentially a kerygmatic, ostensive act in which we point out what God has done and bear witness to His self-revelation, with the intention of focusing people's attention upon God Himself, and of bringing them within 'hearing distance' of His Word that they may hear and believe for themselves. Proclamation that is faithful to the way in which God meets us, in His Word, calls for a corresponding mode of apprehension, the response of faith in which, as Luther puts it, we have to 'stick our eyes in our ears'.

Along with this, however, theological persuasion supplies didactic material: that is, some unfolding of the conceptual content of the divine Word which will provide hearers with an *interpretative framework* to guide their recognition and give their minds some hold upon what they apprehend. It enables them to penetrate into the inherent rationality of the Word so that they may form their

own judgements and yield their rational assent as their minds
come under the power of its inner logic. It cannot be understood
or appropriated from an alien framework, but requires one that
has been developed on the same ground on which knowledge of
God has actually arisen and which is therefore appropriate to it.
To cite St. Thomas, *Deus non est in genere*[1]—He may be understood only out of Himself and through the conceptual content of
His own Word.

These two operations have to be taken together and held
together at two logical levels, for one acts as meta-language to the
other, and neither can be worked into a complete or consistent
system without the other. This is what we have learned in other
fields from Frege and Gödel. We cannot explain clearly what
$2 \times 2 = 4$ means without using word-language and moving on
to a different logical level with its wider syntactical system. Hence,
from the point of view of logical form, the parables of Jesus and
His own reported interpretations belong integrally together, for
the parabolic language of faith-knowledge requires integration
with the wider syntactical formalization provided by the interpretative framework found already in the Gospels, and indeed
apart from the conceptual content of that framework the parables
are not really applicable to existence.

Now we come to the real difficulties with which theological
persuasion has to cope, the fact that in theological knowledge we
are up against a *new way* of thinking, with its own new conceptions and its apposite, if strange, formalization. The assimilation
of what is radically new always involves an arduous struggle, for
we are afraid of breaking logical form and accepting what from
the perspective of prior form inevitably appears a-logical or may
even appear absurd. No one has written about this problem as it
arises within natural science more helpfully than Michael Polanyi
when a new framework arises segregated from any knowledge or
alleged knowledge rooted in different conceptions of experience.
We may cite him at length.

'The two conflicting systems of thought are separated by a
logical gap, in the same sense as a problem is separated from the

[1] *Summa Theologica* 1q.3.5.0; q.4.3. *ad* 1; q.6.2.*ad* 3; q.88.2 *ad* 4; cf. q.30.4 ad 3.

discovery which solves the problem. Formal operations relying on *one* framework of interpretation cannot demonstrate a proposition to persons who rely on *another* framework. Its advocates may not even succeed in getting a hearing from these, since they must first teach them a new language, and no one can learn a new language unless he first trusts that it means something. . . . Proponents of a new system can convince their audience only by first winning their intellectual sympathy for a doctrine they have not yet grasped. Those who listen sympathetically will discover for themselves what they would otherwise never have understood. Such an acceptance is a heuristic process, a self-modifying act, and to this extent a conversion. It produces disciples forming a school, the members of which are separated for the time being by a logical gap from those outside of it.'
And again, from the same page:

'We can now see the great difficulty that may arise in the attempt to persuade others to accept a new idea in science. We have seen that to the extent to which it represents a new way of reasoning, we cannot convince others by formal argument, for so long as we argue within their framework we can never induce them to abandon it. Demonstration must be supplemented, therefore, by forms of persuasion which can induce a conversion. The refusal to enter on the opponent's way of arguing must be justified by making it appear altogether unreasonable.'[1]

The fact that Polanyi has had recourse, to some extent at any rate, to the language of the New Testament, to help him express the difficult process of apprehending and assimilating a new scientific conception is an indication that we do have common factors between scientific and theological persuasion. But what are the supplementary ways of persuasion that theology must use? These are *worship* and *evangelism*. Worship is the exercise of the mind in the contemplation of God in which wonder and awe play an important part in stretching and enlarging our vision, or in opening up our conceptual forms to take in that which by its nature far outruns them. That is why worship goes together with the

---

[1] *Personal Knowledge* (Routledge and Kegan Paul, London, 1958), p. 151.

kerygmatic activity in proclamation whereby we are directed by ostensive acts of reference far beyond ourselves to 'the mighty acts of God'. Polanyi himself speaks of worship as 'heuristic vision'[1]; but it is the same thing, *mutatis mutandis*, that C. F. von Weizsäcker speaks of in science as *meditation* in which we make a transition to a different level of thinking. He describes meditation as 'the process by which consciousness takes possession of a truth in such a way that not only the content but also the structure of consciousness is changed'.[2]

We may reconstruct this by saying that worship is meditation in which we are engaged in heuristic audition, in which we make a transition from the observable to what cannot be observed but may be heard, and from the world of created realities to the Creator Himself. To 'see God' we must renounce the criterion of perceptibility and learn to 'hear' Him, but hear Him in a mode corresponding to the nature of His Word. It is worship that gives our conceptual forms the open texture they require in theological knowledge, and it is prayer that gives our interrogation of divine realities the appropriate mode of 'discovery' in which we do not force God's self-disclosure to conform to our stipulations but find ourselves profoundly questioned before Him. Apart from a 'relation of transcendent reference' which we acquire in worship, everything goes wrong epistemologically, prayer becomes a sort of frustrated soliloquy and knowledge of God is redacted to a form of objectified self-understanding, and we do not even get off the ground, as it were.

But what about *evangelism*, for this too is essential? This is where theological persuasion hurts us, not simply because we are psychologically averse to change and not simply because our prior knowledge and our self-understanding which it enshrines have to be reconstructed to take in the new elements, but because we who stand behind our questioning and who exist in our frameworks of thought are *hostile to the truth of God and require to be reconciled to it*. In every field of knowledge and communication we have to have sympathy with the subject-matter concerned, although this

[1] Op. cit. pp. 280ff.
[2] *The World View of Physics* (Routledge and Kegan Paul, London, 1952), p. 132.

is much more important in the human sciences and above all in
psychology; but in the field of theological knowledge above all,
we have to reckon with the stubborn fact of our deeply ingrained
self-centredness and selfishness which must be torn wide open if
we are to know God in accordance with His nature, that is in
love. This is why theological persuasion must be evangelistic, for
it must show to people that they exist in enmity to the ways of
God and require to 'repent and be converted' if they are to know
the truth. Let it be granted that evangelism is only too often
misused, as it is certainly abused by many, but at its heart evangelism is simply the attempt to *persuade*. It announces the fact that
God was in Christ reconciling the world to Himself, and does not
impute to us our sins but freely offers us forgiveness and love.
And so, as St. Paul expressed it, 'We are ambassadors for Christ,
as though God did beseech you by us; we pray you in Christ's
stead, be ye reconciled to God.' In the passage cited (2 Corinthians
5.20) this is set within an interpretative framework that explains
what is involved and seeks to bring the mind of the reader directly
under the constraint of the love of Christ—that is the logic of
God as He has translated it into our human existence. Evangelists
are not so far wrong when they insist that if we do not believe,
it is not because we cannot but because we do not want to, for
our self-centredness is resistant to the claims of the divine love;
but they are wrong if they play rhetorical tricks upon people's
fears and anxieties and work up their feelings in order to move
them to believe. Yet this is certain, that theological persuasion
cannot succeed without the subsidiary work of moving people
to renounce themselves and leave their inappropriate ways of
thinking, although its primary work is to induce *rational conviction*
and belief in the light of the overwhelming Truth of God as it
is in Jesus Christ.

Index of Persons

Abelard, 101
Altizer, T., 29
Anselm of Canterbury, 21, 101, 170, 180f.
Apel, Karl-Otto, 104
Aquinas, Thomas, 32, 99, 101, 203
Arendt, Hannah, 103
Aristotle, 33; *and see Index of Subjects*
Athanasius, 100, 166
Augustine, 72; *and see Index of Subjects*
Austin, J. L., 23

Bacon, Francis, 35, 41, 93, 197
Barr, J., 46
Barth, Karl, viii, 19, 56, 60, 68f., 76
Berkouwer, G. C., 165
Bohr, N., 14
Bonhoeffer, D., 56, 69, 73ff., 80ff., 85
Buber, M., 29, 40, 47, 106
Bultmann, R., 40, 49ff., 58ff., 67, 77ff., 121
Butler, Joseph, 44

Calvin, John, 31ff., 37, 40, 64, 91, 181; *and see Index of Subjects*
Cicero, Marcus Tullius, 35
Comte, A., 108
Cyprian, 128

Darwin, Charles, 7
Denney, J., 64f.
Dilthey, W., 13, 104
Dirac, P. A. M., 102
Droysen, J. G., 104
Duns Scotus, John, 39, 80, 101

Einstein, A., viii, 10, 14ff., 22, 24, 42, 100, 177

Elsasser, W. M., 14f.
Empie, P. C., 128
Erasmus, Desiderius, 37, 40

Faraday, M., 132
Fermat, P. de, 145
Fraser of Brea, James, 57
Frege, Gottlob, viii, 23f., 46, 203

Galileo Galilei, 7, 124
Gassendi, P., 124
Gödel, Kurt, 100, 203
Gogarten, F., 40

Haeckel, E., 7
Hamilton, W., 29
Hegel, G. W. F., 108
Heidegger, M., 177f.
Heim, Karl, 103
Heinecken, M. J., 128
Heisenberg, W., 7
Henderson, I., 122
Herrmann, W., 108
Hilary of Poitiers, 37
Hitler, A., 73
Hume, David, 44, 197
Hutten, E. H., 119

Johnson, F. E., 107

Kant, I., 41, 53, 129; *and see Index of Subjects*
Kepler, Johannes, 7
Kierkegaard, S., 71, 177
Kuhn, T. S., 46, 106

Laplace, P. S. de, 7
Leo the Great, 128

Index of Subjects

Abstraction, 3, 8, 11, 13, 17, 32f., 90, 102f., 129f., 165, 169, 189, 199
acknowledgement, recognition, 42, 97, 105, 155f., 181ff., 190, 202
activa inquisitio, 35
active reason, 20f., 106
actuality, 13ff., 90ff., 113, 123, 126, 155, 165, 168, 181
adaptation of thought and speech, 19, 101, 116, 157
adequation, 6ff., 11ff., 32, 186f., 198
advance in knowledge, viii, 4ff., 18, 72, 89, 106, 111, 118, 120, 132, 200, 202
aesthetics, 93, 105
analogy, 24f., 80
Anglicanism, 57, 126, 130
anthropology, 53
anthropocentricity, 68, 109
anxiety, vii, 5, 120, 159, 162, 206
Apollinarianism, 142
apophatic thought, 22
a posteriori thought, 89, 99, 102, 197
apostles, apostolic foundation, 59, 128, 152
applicability, 7, 16, 24, 42, 77, 151, 203
a priori thought, 90, 92, 129f.
Archimedian point, 102
Arianism, 30f.
Aristotelianism, 90, 101f., 123ff., 129, 148
ascension of Christ, 126f., 158
assent, 42, 61, 101, 147, 153, 155ff., 195, 202f.
astronomy, 29, 93
atheism, 31, 69
atonement, 50, 55, 63f., 143ff., 172
Augustinianism, 21, 103, 108, 124f.

authority, 61, 68, 73f., 76, 89f., 101, 156, 191
autonomy, 69, 90, 162
awe, 11, 16, 42, 196
axioms, axiomatic thinking, 15, 99ff., 110, 133

Baptism, 70, 158, 160
beauty, intellectual, viii, 112
Bible, Scriptures, 19, 35, 37f., 39, 67, 74, 79, 85, 107, 109, 120f., 143f., 148f., 156, 181, 203
biblical thought, 32, 35, 39, 120f., 128, 147ff., 151f., 184, 203
biology, 14, 53

Calvinism, 57
Cartesian thought, 18, 20, 50f., 103, 108
cataleptic apprehension, 22, 97
cataphatic thought, 22, 25, 125, 128
catholicity, 125
cause, causality, 7, 11, 23, 39, 58, 104, 106, 109, 129, 131, 138, 177, 198
celestial mechanics, 7
certainty, 8, 16
chemistry, 14, 43, 53
Christianity, historic, 3, 47, 50f., 149
Christocentricity, 60ff., 76f.
Christology, 30, 63f., 74, 77f., 126f.
Church, vii, 3, 30, 35, 56, 71, 74, 85, 106, 111, 113, 117, 121ff., 130, 138, 148, 150, 152f., 159, 190, 192
cognitive tools, instruments, viii, 3f., 11, 19, 43, 104, 117, 120, 133, 140, 147, 175
coherence, 45, 90, 94f., 104, 110, 132ff.